STRENGTH OF THE OAK
STRENGTH OF THE WILLOW

How to Find
Courage & Compassion
in a Turbulent World

BY ANDREW L. ANDERSON

STRENGTH OF THE OAK
STRENGTH OF THE WILLOW
How to Find Courage & Compassion in a Turbulent World

Copyright © 2023 by Andrew L. Anderson

Inspired Legacy Publishing is a division of (DBA) Inspired Legacy, LLC
PO Box 900816
Sandy UT 84090-0816.

All Bible verses are KJV.

ISBN 979-8-9872471-0-5 (paperback)
ISBN 979-8-9872471-1-2 (hardcover)

Printed in the United States of America

What People Are Saying

"Absolutely one of my favorite personal development books of all time!"
—*Bridget Cook-Burch, New York Times & Wall Street Journal Best-selling Author, Transformational Trainer & Passionate Humanitarian*

"The learnings and tools that you will acquire from reading and internalizing this written treasure will help you grow and truly live into your greatest potential."
—*Kevin Hall, International best-selling author of "Aspire: Discovering Your Purpose through the Power of Words."*

"He makes the complicated simple; which is what great leaders do. He provides a well thought out and proven recipe for breaking destructive habits and plumbs the depths to show how transformation is truly possible."
—*Jake Proffitt, Kingdom Consulting LLC*

"Strength of the Oak, Strength of the Willow is like a ray of sunshine for both mind and soul."
—*Sophie Rouméas, Mindful Therapies (Hypnosis & Systemic Constellation), Coach Mindfulness & Meditation*

"Inspiration, self-reflection and hope…Strength of the Oak, Strength of the Willow delivers."
— *Maureen Ryan Blake, Maureen Ryan Blake Media Productions*

"This book is an outstanding teaching tool! …Andrew's ability to be vulnerable, seek feedback from others, and continually grow is inspiring!"
—*Deborah Wiener, Author, Speaker, Entrepreneur*

Dedication

To my chosen family: Chandler and Tanner.
You know why.

And to my forever family: My parents, siblings,
in-laws, nieces and nephews
and my beloved wife and children.
May the heritage of our roots and our abundant
branches always connect us in love.

Contents

A Note from the Author

Thank you, sincerely, for picking up this book. You're taking a leap of faith as you dive into this work. I recognize that you're entrusting me with the privilege of joining you on your journey of genuine self-improvement. Believe me, I don't take that lightly. In fact, it means the world to me.

Even as you read this, we are engulfed in soul-wrenching pain on this planet. While the solutions are right here at our fingertips, too often they feel so far out of reach. Many of us haven't been led to what our next step is because we cannot see through the chaotic darkness to the joy and power on the other side. What I present to you is a light in that dark, along with simple steps teaching you how to produce your own luminosity, brilliance and radiance by tapping into the *greatest* source of light, ever.

I'm sharing the truths, principles and values that I've learned from the greatest sages throughout time. The Christian perspective, which I cherish, is founded upon one of the greatest teachers who ever lived. He carried the courageous strength of an oak, the compassionate strength of a willow, and the cumulative force of every other tree he created. These God-given, precious pearls of wisdom, carefully applied, have transformed and brought renewal to my life.

From early adolescence all the way through to my adult professional endeavors, I've answered a call to become a compelling speaker, a master teacher and trainer (both in and out of the classroom), a community and spiritual leader, a trusted mentor and a certified life-transformation and business-productivity coach. There have been thousands along the way whom I have been privileged to serve and humbled to witness as they've passed through their very own personal and powerful transformative experiences. And now, it's your turn.

Over the years, dozens of clients, at the end of their rope, have come to me in desperation and defeatism and said, "I don't know where to turn! All the counselors and therapists have waiting lists. And I need help *now* for me or my spouse or my child or my friend." People are hurting from deep places of pain–mentally, emotionally and spiritually. Faith is faltering. Fears are found at every turn. And today, we need leaders who inspire and words that heal. This is a book that will build you as that leader for your tribe, family, relationship, marriage, friends, businesses, places of worship and nations.

But leaders, like you and me, are not just whisked away from the grueling valleys of dejection and magically placed upon mountain peaks of triumph. There is no "Easy Street" nor is there a secret mode of teleportation to the top. Each progressive step must be earned and owned--each life lesson learned, individually and oh so personally.

My path has been surprisingly rocky and unexpectedly dimmer than I'd hoped for. My lows nearly caused everything to cave in all around me. The tears of hopelessness flowed frequently and my vision was often blurred, making each step seem impossible. The loneliness, depression and feelings of worthlessness wreaked havoc in my soul. I didn't know if I'd make it out alive. My legacy seemed to be approaching a demoralizing dead end.

Why do I choose to throw open the front door of my life in vulnerability and share all of this with you? It's because I now carry a steady hope and I am a witness that God's goodness is available to any and all who are willing to exercise the slightest bit of faith. I learned I wasn't alone. Help seemed to pop up out of nowhere. Light appeared gradually and at times, suddenly.

It all worked out for a wounded man like me. It works out for my clients. I know it can work for you too.

However, it takes strength unlike any other to keep this brilliance burning. Too many so-called strengths may appear solid, steady and strong, but they cannot endure under severe stress. What is needed now, more than ever, are infallible practices and principles that last through the ages. These are timeless, rooted verities that you can absolutely count on, with truths that uplift you, challenge and support you, rather than the winds that buffet your branches about or attempt to knock you down.

This book is meant to be an answer, a balm of healing for our pain. I invite you to read slowly, as if I were here with you right now. Join me in a conversation as I share some stories, ask a few deep questions and invite you to consider your ways and perhaps make some slight but oh, so powerful, tweaks.

There will be simple yet profound exercises that I ask you to engage in and ironclad tools to empower your success. Please take the Journal Entries to heart. These moments of reflection will solidify your learnings in a meaningful way. As you bring your A-game, and give yourself the effort you deserve, each invitation to go a little bit deeper will reveal parts of you that are ready to shine. You'll discover new life, all kinds of possibilities and far-reaching meaning for your existence.

Take your time. Enjoy the process. And again, I'm grateful beyond measure for the honor to be with you on your own personal pilgrimage.

With courage and compassion,
Andrew L. Anderson

CHAPTER ONE

Grounded

*"Each human being is bred with a unique set of
potentials that yearn to be fulfilled as surely as the
acorn yearns to become the oak within it."*
—Aristotle

Grounded. What could be worse for a nine-year-old kid than the parental sentencing of being banished to your room? No friends. No TV. No video games. No bike riding. No fun at all. And there I was, miserable and grounded.

I knew I was in the wrong. We were on the playground and my "friend" from across the street asked me to hold down a fellow fourth grade, Dallas Cowboys fan while we gave him a dead-leg (a simple and yet painful knee to the hamstring, causing a deadening sensation and a terrible bruise). It wasn't nice, I know. My one and only disgraceful visit to the principal's office, as a bully, came because I was a die-hard San Francisco 49ers fan. And, ooh, in 1994, the Cowboys and Niners were fire and ice.

Still, I'll never forget the sound of my mom's piercing voice over that heavy, black office phone on the day I thought my life was over, "You'll never see the light of day again!" Now, whether those words legitimately came out of my mother's mouth or not is to this very day denied and debated, but that's precisely what my guilty, juvenile ears heard. . .loud and clear. Needless to say, it was a long walk home that afternoon.

Glancing ahead, two decades down this road of life, to my chagrin, I found myself once again, grounded. But this time I was staring my thirtieth year in the face, in the basement bathroom mirror of my parents' house. I looked into my sullen eyes, deep in despair and disbelief.

Am I really the stereotypical thirty-year-old son living in his retired parents' basement?

Yep!

I shook my head slowly as the weight of my shame-filled predicament brought my gaze down. My eyes closed as I fought back ugly tears of humiliation. What could be worse for a grown man than being banished to his parents' house? No wife. No kids. No job. No fun. And there I was, disgustedly divorced and grounded, ironically, again in my parents' basement.

I took all the blame for my marriage that had ended after seven remarkable years, three of the most beautiful little girls this world has ever seen, divinely precious and unforgettable memories of love, learning and laughter, along with a lot of tears and trials, hardship and headaches.

That marriage was supposed to last forever. The thought of our family being broken up had never, not once, crossed my mind. To me it was not even an option. Through thick and thin, whatever it took, I'd always believed that with enough faith, God would bring help and healing to my heartfelt prayers.

Those prayers were being answered in ways that were imperceptible, at the time, to my mortal eyes. In that blur, it felt like everything had come crashing down like a cabinet full of fine china onto a hard tile floor. The hallowed pieces of what I cherished most, my marriage and family, had been shattered and scattered in every possible direction.

At that rock bottom, soul-wrenching moment of my life, there was a profound choice that had to be made: would I suffocate myself by burying my head in the ground and give up on me, my girls, and my God. . .or would I stand up and plant deep, firm roots as far down as possible, drawing from a source of life-saving, divine sustenance?

Half sitting, half lying in the bed of a cold basement, lit only by a small lamp in the far corner of my "room," I kept a sturdy grip on a hardbound book, propped up by my knees. I ran my fingers over the imprinted words on the denim blue cover: *Man's Search For Meaning.* I opened it up one more time to read the words that swirled in my mind from my never-met-hero and mentor, Nazi concentration camp survivor, Viktor Frankl:[1]

"There were always choices to make. Every day, every hour, offered the opportunity to make a decision, a decision which determined whether you would or would not submit to those powers which threatened to rob you of your very self, your inner freedom; which determined whether or not you would become the plaything of circumstance, renouncing freedom and dignity to become molded into the form of the typical inmate."

I put the book down beside me and laid my head fully back onto the welcoming pillow, allowing my shoulders and spine to relax. As I looked up at the dark shadows on the white plastered ceiling, my mind wandered back to this roller coaster of a ride I'd been on.

My wife and I had been working diligently with our counselor for nearly four years, doing everything we knew to find peace and answers to prayers. I'm a "give it everything you've got" kind of guy and I was fighting like my life depended on it. Despite all our attempts to resolve the conflicts, she didn't see how it could work and decided that we should separate.

Within the matter of a short month, we welcomed a precious new baby girl, moved to another state, and then separated. I had to leave my teaching position, which faded out of my dreams right along with the marriage that I had always believed was indestructible. This bitter aftertaste felt like it was never going away. The devastation of losing everything that I'd planned for, dreamed, worked, sacrificed and loved for rocked my world in a horrific way. I had pathetically failed my wife, my daughters and my Creator who had gifted me this precious family. *How can they, how can He, ever trust me again? Can I trust Him? I put all my faith in you, Father, and now look at me!* I could hardly look anyone in the eye...much less my God.

---

[1] Viktor E. Frankly (2014). "Man's Search for Meaning", p.62, Beacon Press, Boston

During the following six months, I diligently strove to restore what had been broken, but all of my efforts were to no avail. As I was handed those heavy divorce papers, on what was supposed to be a beautifully redemptive Easter Sunday with our little family, I found myself in a new and unfamiliar place, filled with a mental, emotional and spiritual darkness. I was suffocating at the bottom of a pit that I thought I might not ever crawl out of, a prison where I'd be serving a life-sentence, and some. *Why is this happening to me?*

I was brought back to the present moment as a touch of light filtered into my parents' basement windows with that book still beside me. *I am not okay.* Depression, anxiety, rage, confusion, loneliness. . . You name it, I felt it. *How in the world did I end up here?* My hope was hanging by a thread. Sometimes that thread looked like it was done for and sometimes it felt like God was bolstering it into an unbreakable iron rod. Honestly, I didn't know up from down. I was all over the place.

After seven grueling months of dependent living, I moved out of my parents' home and into my own one-bedroom apartment. I thought I was on the brink of a new life, but in less than a year of solitude in my new abode, my 100% commission career in real estate left me with nine bucks in my bank account and a few thousand in debt to a selfless sister and caring brother. They had graciously loaned me enough to pay my last month's rent along with my commitment to uphold my child support.

There I was, divorced and in despair. Now completely broke and broken. Unforgivable. Lost. Grieving. Unworthy. Sunk. *God, how is this fair? I did everything I could. Where are the miracles? Why can't You just fix this?* I was furious with myself, with my wife who would no longer carry that title, and with my Father above.

With my head hung low, ready to roll right off, I packed my things and moved back in with my parents, again. I hadn't even been divorced for a year and somehow, to my dismay, I was right back where I'd started. *Enough is enough! This is pathetic.* I drew a line in the sand. I decided it was time to deal with all of the demons that clouded my mind and spirit as I earnestly questioned every possible way to get past all of the head and heart trash that was beating me down to a pulp. Something had to change.

Sick and tired of dragging myself through this despicable muck, I pulled my head out. I stood up and wiped my healing tears from my eyes so I could finally see. I threw off the rusty chains of my self-induced prison. With God's enabling grace and my own outright conviction, I made a choice to defy those powers that were threatening to rob me of my inner freedom. *I will win this inner war! Death by doubt is not how I'm going down.* I planted my roots. I grounded myself to my Source, ready to grow.

From the time of that commitment, unexpected angels began entering my life. There was a neighborhood friend of my parents, who happened to be a highly skilled psychologist, who began meeting with me on a regular basis. He helped restore my dignity.

My four older siblings, who never gave up on me, sat through countless sob stories. They were the greatest support system that could only do what family does best--love...no matter what.

A new boss offered me a job to join her leadership team as a coach. She had seen my work ethic in sales and understood my ability to connect in the classroom as a teacher. After a vulnerable meeting in her office where I tearfully poured my heart and all of my challenges upon her, she called the next morning at 7:00 a.m. and said, "Andrew, I'm making up a new job for you." She saw a glimpse of the greatness within me and sent me down the coaching path that I so deeply revered. Thank you, Stacie.

New friends spent tender time teaching me, through example, how to squeeze joy out of life through recreation and meaningful connection. Another compassionate coach offered to work with me for free. A mentor lit a fire inside me that continues to fuel me at a more meaningful level today. Those earthly angels led me through an utter abyss as they patiently applauded my personal transformation, as slow as it may have seemed to me. God had not given up and neither would I.

As a teacher, I had always been attracted to powerful resources, but now I became an absolute sponge to all things self-improvement—books, audiobooks, seminars, classes, workshops, retreats, whatever I could find.

Most importantly, I recommitted myself to the faith that had helped me survive, seeking to serve others and flee my pity party of one. I went back to my roots, to the values, principles and practices that had allowed me to soar upward for so many years, until this startling dark night of my soul.

In return, God's loving kindness was more than enough to buoy me up and out of the hellish hole I found myself in. He planted a seed in my soul. I was going to be grounded now in an entirely different way. He had a new and glorious gift, one more culminating angel who was absolutely perfect...for me. It all started after a Sunday family dinner when my older sister created a profile for me on an online dating site.

No way! Not me. I don't think so.

Sisters are persuasive. It didn't take more than one week for her to get me to start browsing. "Hey, look at this one, little bro. She's so cute!" With my arm twisted, I sent a message. Mystery girl sent one back. We set up a time to talk on the phone. That hour-long conversation turned into a nightly routine of putting kids to bed, going outside, and either lying on the trampoline while gazing up at the stars or walking slowly around the neighborhood, unable to put the phone down. This is where I learned to love again. The three hundred miles and state borders were not enough to hold our hearts apart.

She came my way for the first few dates on our kickoff weekend together. I then traveled south to see her as soon as I got the chance. We alternated like this for a couple months. She (and miraculously her mother too) believed that they had struck gold. Oddly enough, I decided to start believing them. Chari (pronounced like "sorry" with a "sh"), my sweetheart of a rock, became my most cherished confidant, supportive companion and eventually, I'm humbled to say, my beautiful wife–for all of which I'd *never* be sorry. Fortunately for me, she saw the absolute best in me. Her inspiration does wonders for my hopes and dreams to this day.

Chari had two phenomenal kids of her own. I became their primary father figure and this renewed my faith in the ability to be a man again. We created a human together, a little boy who carries the best of both his mom and me. I stepped back into a commission role as I built a coaching business of my own, which I've refined and grown over the last seven years. Chari and the kids and I moved into our dream home that I previously would have never believed could have been mine.

I continued the path of learning and growth that showed me how to change my beliefs at the deepest level of unconsciousness, all the way down to my neural pathways. I began doing this work for others in my coaching sessions. I saw miraculous results as I carefully guided my clients through their own dark nights of the soul and into the light of their unique and purposeful paths.

Patterns began developing right before my eyes. It was as if Divinity was opening the windows of heaven, illuminating what holds each of us back from finding a fulfilling life of freedom and coming to congruence with our higher selves.

I could see it so clearly. Even through my healing and growth, negative emotions I knew as resentment, anger, sadness, fear, desire to control, blame, guilt and shame had haunted me for way too long. These feelings lingered toward myself and my previous wife. Limiting beliefs about my core value in this world, my ability to live out my Life Mission and my overall worthiness before God had all been in jeopardy for far too long.

With rejuvenated vision, I continued taking steps to overcome, stronger now as I brought others with me. Just like I had discovered, this roller coaster of life is much more profound and enjoyable when we have someone we love and trust sitting right next to us. We're locked and loaded, hand in hand, ready for every gut-wrenching drop, tight turn, accelerated climb, unexpected giggle and insuppressible scream that bring such excitement and uncertainty, joy and jubilation, all the way up to the moment we roll to a stop and safely plant our feet on solid ground.

It's funny, isn't it, how a word like grounded can have such a strong positive or negative connotation? Where did that come from, anyway? I discovered that parents started using the word around the year 1940. For a decade or so before this, pilots, who had been disciplined for misconduct, were justifiably denied certain privileges, unable to fly, and therefore "grounded."[2] I guess it seemed fitting for kids too!

As I went back a bit further, though, I found a fifteenth-century definition of "grounded" as a "source, origin, or cause." And in the thirteenth century, it was used as a "sense of reason, a motive."[3] With this insight, being grounded is actually a positive connection to what motivates us. It's a compelling reason that comes from a deep source.

I am able to now reflect on that defining time of my life, my grounding. What I see, with almost perfect clarity, is how that place of perceived imprisonment became a solid bedrock where I learned who I was, what I really wanted and why. I've heard it said that when we hit rock bottom, it's a great place to build a strong foundation. So maybe getting grounded isn't such a bad thing after all. It just so happened to be exactly what I needed. What about you? Have you been hitting rock bottom in any areas of your life? Is it time to ground yourself?

It all starts with an inner desire, and an untapped strength that I promise you will find. I call it the **Strength of the Oak**. But first, we look to creation to heal us, and to provide crucial, life-saving and transformational lessons that are simple and yet deeply profound. I invite you, dare you and challenge you to go on this journey with me. Are you ready?

---

[2] https://www.etymonline.com/word/grounded
[3] https://www.etymonline.com/word/ground

CHAPTER TWO

Roots and Wings

*"Change your opinions, keep to your principles;
change your leaves, keep intact your roots."*
—*Victor Hugo*

We don't have to look much further than our own backyard, a nearby park or perhaps a quick online search to observe nature teaching us master classes on getting grounded. Take a look at the mighty oak tree.

Since ancient times, the oak has been praised for its legendary strength, durability, longevity and exceptional properties for wood-working. These trees have become objects of art, mythology and even worship. The oak is the national tree or symbol of several countries, including England, America, Cyprus, France, Germany, Jordan, Poland, Romania and Wales.[4]

As if that wasn't powerful enough, ships and baseball bats, chariots and drumsticks, coffins and cutting boards have all been made from oak trees. The oak has been life and lifestyle sustaining in a myriad of powerful ways.[5]

What is it about these natural wonders that makes them so valuable and stoic?

- Size: They can grow to over one hundred feet tall and more than nine feet in diameter.
- Age: Some oak trees have been known to live thousands of years.
- Defense system: Tannic acid is found in the acorns and leaves, which helps to guard from insects and fungi. It's even poisonous to livestock and larger animals.

---

[4] https://en.wikipedia.org/wiki/Oak
[5] https://en.wikipedia.org/wiki/Oak

- Density: It is an extremely hard and strong wood.
- Last but not least (and most impressive to me): The remarkable root system.[6]

At the beginning of an oak's life, when an acorn first sprouts, most of its energy is spent on root development, with little growth above ground. The initial root is called a taproot, which grows deep underground, seeking a dependable supply of moisture. Once this is accomplished, greater foliage and branch growth can begin.

Soon the taproot is surpassed by an extensive root system which spreads horizontally. This lateral mass of roots will bring the tree moisture and nutrients for the entirety of its lifetime. Most oak tree roots lie only eighteen inches under the soil. They may spread, though, to occupy a space four to seven times the width of the tree's crown. The other wonder is that when two of these majestic oak trees of the same species grow side by side, they can even share root systems that have grafted together. Now we're talking serious strength and stability! [7]

The combination of such an extensively grounded root system and environmentally protective defense system creates the perfect harmony for this noble and worthy giant of a tree, the oak.[8]

Strength of the Oak: Courage

There's got to be something for us humans to emulate from this marvel of a creation. Think about it. What if we were to send our taproots deep to original, nurturing sources of meaning and motivation? Imagine the storms of life we could courageously conquer with roots so wide they become even bigger than we are. Roots that reach out and graft to our same species, our fellow travelers on this mortal sojourn. What could happen with that kind of connection? Think of the possibilities!

---

[6] https://en.wikipedia.org/wiki/Oak
[7] https://homeguides.sfgate.com/root-system-oak-trees-48319.html
[8] https://homeguides.sfgate.com/root-system-oak-trees-48319.html

But how? And is sheer strength enough? What about when we feel strong and yet we still break? You know, those moments when we're certain we're doing what's right and we simply won't back down and then. . .snap. What about then? I knew there had to be more, so I set out to find more answers, some kind of balance.

Strength of the Willow: Compassion

One day while reading from Wayne W. Dyer's *Change Your Thoughts Change Your Life*, I stumbled upon this most enlightening passage. The classic Chinese text, *Tao Te Ching*, is credited to the sixth century BC philosopher and author Lao Tzu. The seventy-six verse reads:

"All things, including grass and trees,
are soft and pliable in life;
dry and brittle in death.

Stiffness is thus a companion of death;
flexibility a companion of life....
A tree that cannot bend
will crack in the wind.

The hard and stiff will be broken;
the soft and supple will prevail."

As I consider the trees that are most willing to bend, I can't help but think of the simple and sober willow. With the wind passing through its leaves and branches, it resembles a ballerina—graceful, flowing, poetic and fluent in essence. Such a gentle tree might seem weak and powerless, and herein lies the great paradox.

Willow trees have long been known for their unique and favorable properties. Ancient texts speak of using the willow bark and other chemicals found within for treatment of fevers and headaches. In our modern era, a connection to the development of aspirin is also present.

During WWII, troops received much needed supplies from British airplanes that dropped baskets made from willows branches. Charcoal is produced from the willow and used as an artistic medium, as well as an energy resource. It has also served as a source of food; the inner bark is edible, either raw or cooked. The leaves and underground shoots can also be eaten. In manufacturing, whistles and wands, boxes and brooms, rope and paper all are produced from the willow.

Many cultures revere this hallowed tree, including Jewish feasts and festivals. In Buddhism, the willow branch is chiefly attributed to the goddess of compassion. Christian churches in Europe often use the branches in place of palms to celebrate Palm Sunday. In China, willow branches are placed on gates and entryway doors to help ward off wandering evil spirits. And Ukraine has chosen the willow to be its national tree.

One of the most unique and mesmerizing characteristics of willows is their environmental contribution. They are used for wildlife habitat and windbreak. Willows are regularly planted on the slopes and the borders of streams to prevent soil erosion. Their roots are often larger than the stem from whence they grow, providing a phenomenally strong support system.[9]

The willow possesses a toughness and tenacity incomparable to that of the oak. It's a quietly dignified, almost illusive strength, like Mother Teresa or Gandhi. There is no pomp, no vanity. It's a "here am I, take me as I am" kind of strength. It's the power some dogs possess. You know, those adorable puppy eyes that coerce you into giving them attention and affection, even when you don't want to. It's submissive strength. And it works.

The willow's gift is found in its ability to embrace a storm with open arms. As wind whips through, the willow stays grounded, moving *with* rather than against the storm. It has learned that such battles may not

---

[9] Info from the last four paragraphs comes from https://en.wikipedia.org/wiki/Willow

be worth the fight. "Sticks and stones may break my bones, but wind will never hurt me," it says. . .whispering, of course. This wisdom provides the willow with the means to enjoy the sunshine and warmth of beautiful days. It's not compelled to squander time and energy resisting the nasty ones.

Surely we could all learn to be a bit more like the unruffled willow tree, couldn't we? What if we were to compassionately allow others' actions, opinions and beliefs to pass through with a welcoming ease? Imagine life's tempests that could be tamed with the matched willingness of a willow? Maybe people in our lives would simply give in like a loving dog owner melting over those irresistible puppy eyes? What would we be capable of if we possessed powers like that?

But how? And is such flexibility sustainable forever? What if I bend so much I break? You know, those moments when we give and give and give and then just can't give anymore? What about then? There's got to be more to it, right? After all the studying I'd done and connections to personal events in my life I saw, I discovered something amazing: there *is* a balance.

Strength of the Oak *AND* Strength of the Willow

There's a powerful synergy created when the counterbalancing principles of the **Strength of the Oak** and the **Strength of the Willow** join forces. What I present in this book is all about finding a complementary relationship with both.

These strengths don't care about what pronoun we identify with or who we choose to love. I believe that each human carries these qualities in the innermost parts of our DNA, but it's important to know how to foster them into *actual* strengths. We must learn and practice how to utilize them to overcome the daily challenges of life and the bigger, more complex issues each individual faces.

Stephen Covey brilliantly taught us:

"Synergy is everywhere in nature. If you plant two plants close together, the roots comingle and improve the quality of the soil so that both plants will grow better than if they were separated. If you put two pieces of wood together, they will hold much more than the total weight held by each separately. The whole is greater than the sum of its parts."[10]

When we achieve this kind of synergy, magic happens. And the moment this unrivaled magic makes its mark, the finished product leaves us grounded, yet flexible. Our level of commitment is 110% —we're all in and still willing, if necessary, to surrender and set it all aside. We experience total justice matched with unconditional mercy. High hopes exist along with a forgiving heart when we and others fall short. Could the letter of the law (obedience to the *T*) and the spirit of the law (benevolent reverence) be simultaneously fulfilled?

This synergy grants us the competency to say 'no' to life's noisy non-essentials while being open to a 'yes!' when we hear abundance surprisingly knocking on our door. It reveals a relentless drive on the inside coupled with a kind demeanor on the outside. We are able to receive God's all-enveloping love and just as easily and powerfully turn right around to freely give that love back to ourselves and others. We are proud and still humble, anchored but untethered.

In our interactions with others there's a concisely calculated candor along with unquestionable care. We experience personal and interpersonal power, which leaves us unshakeable, yet willing to shift. We discover an immunity to the negative criticism found in the barrage of opinions that seek to unravel us and also an open acceptance of the constructive feedback that beckons to build us. What's left is a creative, exuberant energy while graciously carrying a penetrating peace.

This synergistic **Strength of the Oak** and **Strength of the Willow** is here for you, ready to be unveiled.

---

[10] Stephen R. Covey (2012). "The Wisdom and Teachings of Stephen R. Covey", p.84, Simon and Schuster

I can promise that as you fully engage in this book, soaking in every ounce of applicable knowledge and wisdom through the empowering stories I present and the practical tools I offer, you will walk away with a riveted courage unlike any other your heart has ever known. You will find uncommon compassion that will beckon you to lead, love and serve our bleeding world. A dormant power of personal freedom and potential that you've always longed for is awaiting you.

Wherever you might fall on the multitude of life's never-ending journeys, **I invite you to embark on this inner adventure with yourself and see what's yearning to ignite. Let loose the Life Mission that's been calling you for way too long. Become the absolute best version of you that this world so desperately needs. *It's time.* You deserve this.**

Not only is it vital, but it is absolutely possible for a person to possess both the **Strength of the Oak** and the differing, complementary **Strength of the Willow**. These are not superpowers that are independent of each other. I never liked being told that I couldn't have my cake and eat it too. You certainly can fly like Wonder Woman, have heat vision like Superman, and spidey-sense like Spiderman all at the same time! Your belief in the ability to build these strengths side by side is precisely where we must begin to launch into what's possible for you.

Let me tell you about a man who's married these two principles about as perfectly as I've ever seen. His name is Trevor Bell.

It was back to school time, September of 2009. I was a young, confident, newly hired teacher at a private, seminary institution, prepared to take on religious education with high school kids. We were ready to dive in and study ancient scripture and apply it to their teenage lives with hopes of changing the trajectory of their future.

Trevor Bell was the principal of more than nine hundred enrolled students and seven teachers. I had just witnessed this good-looking, muscular, radiant, spiritual giant do a standing backflip in the halls of our building. Earlier that day, he was doing the moonwalk and other perfectly impersonated dance moves that Michael Jackson introduced to the world. The students ate it up!

This old man (who wasn't even forty), dressed in a suit and tie, had completely blown their minds with how "not stuffy" he actually was. He had won their hearts, plain and simple. In four fast years, Trevor modeled for me what I now know to be an ideal **Strength of the Oak** and **Strength of the Willow** synergy.

I'll never forget the day a seventeen-year-old kid thought it was okay to curse me out in front of twenty-five of his classmates. With all the self-restraint my boiling head could summon, I bit my tongue, walked into principal Bell's office and told him of the situation at hand.

I watched in amazement at his prevailing presence alone. Without a single finger being laid on this teen, he verbally picked that punk up off of his feet, pinned him against the wall and set him straight. Trevor's self-control and precision mirrored that of a surgeon's scalpel, sharp and carefully guided to get the job done, no more, no less. **Strength of the Oak.**

On another, less testosterone-filled day, I went through the wringer with an even higher authority, an administrator who oversaw all new hires in their first few years of teaching. This gentleman was a letter of the law, by the book, kind of leader. In fact, I began to wonder if he was *writing* the book. When he walked through the front door of our building, we'd jokingly whisper, "The eagle has landed. The eagle has landed."

He had just finished observing one of my classes and felt it was his job to humble me by putting me in my place in that classroom. He ran through a list that seemed a mile long of all the "constructive criticisms" that would help refine my rougher edges, the ones that eventually would get ironed out with experience. I was indeed humbled, and a bit downtrodden.

Looking back, his critique was probably spot on, and yet I wasn't grounded or confident enough at that time to see it. I hung my head a bit lower than needed as I slowly sulked into Trevor's office and shared the list. He empathetically listened, reassured me that I was being a bit too hard on myself by taking it personally, built me up and sent me on my way to prepare for my next class.

Trevor asked if he could watch me teach the following day. We sat down afterward and he slid over a list that looked something like this:

10 Things to Improve

1. _____
2. _____
3. _____
4. _____
5. _____
6. _____
7. _____
8. _____
9. _____
10. Nothing! Amazing lesson, Andrew! You are blessing so many of these students' lives! Keep it up. ☺

That note picked me up at a time when my head was hanging so low I thought I'd never be able to pull it up off the floor. His tender love and encouragement were precisely what I needed that day. He heard much more behind my words of complaint; he had listened to my heart. **Strength of the Willow**.

People like Trevor Bell are mesmerizing to me, not just in how they carry themselves, but also in how they make others feel. They possess a simple gift that helps you know that they know exactly where they're at in their life. There's no question as to their standards or values. They are who they are and the wake of their actions proves it. It's attractive leadership.

When you sit down with someone like this, you don't wonder, *Are they coming from a place of integrity? Are they who they say they are? Can I trust this person?* You just know. And that knowing invites you in—to be honest, to be vulnerable, and to share what you don't share with anyone else.

This kind of synergy that exists when a centered and accepting friend gives you their listening ear allows you to offer them your heart. Healing takes place. Hope is lifted.

As this world spins faster and faster and the noise and commotion gets louder and louder, there is an even greater call for leaders who can bring us through these blinding, deafening dust storms.

Hearts are failing. Courage is waning. Faith is needed.

And so, the call rings on, waiting to be answered.

Vertical Roots: *Raison d'être*

Remember that part, earlier, where we learned about the oak's tap-root? From the onset, that taproot drives down, seeking a deep and dependable water supply. This happens before any lateral roots develop, before the tiny sprout grows into a solid trunk and before beautiful foliage and acorns are produced. Finding that source of water is the number one priority for a guaranteed future of longevity.

In the "Sermon on the Mount," Jesus taught a large group of followers, "Blessed are they which do hunger and thirst after righteousness: for they shall be filled" (Matthew 5:6).

The oak's taproot has that compelling thirst and so must we. You'll know it's been quenched when you find that *sense of reason and motive*. There's a resonance with your *source, origin and cause*. You're grounded and you know it. Without it, you'll always feel empty, like something's missing. No matter the amount of money you make, the fun you have, or the prestigious positions you hold, it'll never be enough. It's the fried fluff that never fulfills—Twinkies instead of potatoes.

My experience of coaching hundreds of adults over the last eight years—and being surrounded by incredible humans my entire life—has led me to the sad realization that the majority of them have yet to discover their *raison d'être*, a purpose-driven mission for their life. It's like we've got a generation or two who have sadly been raised on figurative Twinkies, being told what to do and think, never owning where they're going or why and bellyaching about everything and everyone around them. There's a tremendous lack of direction and drive. We've got forests of people falling flat on their faces, lacking principle-based values that are essential to sustain them through life's rugged terrain.

I used to be totally and completely oblivious to this elusive pandemic. I sincerely believed that most people knew exactly why they were here on this earth. It wasn't until a few years ago that I began to appreciate just how fortunate I had been to have what so many were missing. I guess I had simply taken for granted a very personal and sacred experience that took place at the age of fourteen.

Fourteen is hard! You've been a teenager for over a year. Your body is awkward (at least mine was). Friends and pimples come and go every week. Teachers, parents and coaches all seem to have a different opinion about how you should live your life and none of them are holding it back. The media barrages you with distorted models of so-called "happiness." And that untouchable crush you dream of being with always seems just…out…of…reach.

That's what I experienced. I was lost and lonely. I was waking up at 5:00 a.m. for a daily paper route on my rollerblades and then going to an early morning seminary class at 6:40 a.m. before the regular school day started. I begrudgingly played football with a bunch of knuckleheads after school and then headed home for dinner and homework. And then I'd wake up and do it all again.

I had friends, kind of. They were in the grade below me and attended a different school. I hated sitting with my teammates at lunch, as they participated in your run-of-the-mill, shallow, teenage "guy talk" that just didn't make me feel very dignified inside. So, I often found myself walking around the halls during lunch and breaks, pretending like I was going somewhere, so as not to be seen as a loner.

I'll never forget discreetly strolling into the bathroom one day during lunch. Stepping over to the largest stall, I slowly pushed open that cold, metal, maroon door. As I slid the shiny stainless-steel latch into a locked position, my greatest yearning was to shut out the depressing world that felt so foreign to me. *How long can I stay in here? What if this is my only sanctuary?*

I stepped up onto the toilet seat. I didn't want anyone to see my shoes and be able to later identify the loser who was running away to cry in the bathroom. That throne of solitude felt awkwardly comfortable for the remainder of our lunch period. My tears turned from sadness to disgust. I hated myself. *Why can't I be like everyone else? Will I ever fit in? How long am I going to have to feel like an alien on my own home planet?*

Finally, I'd had enough.

I shared some of my struggles with my loving parents and they helped me prepare to receive a guiding, comforting and protecting blessing, inspired by my Heavenly Father above. This blessing would come as a patriarch (spiritual leader within my church) laid his hands on my head and spoke divinely guided words of confidence, fortitude and reassurance. My preparation for this special day included fasting, prayer and diligent study.

My efforts and pleading with my Maker had paid off. The inspired words of counsel illuminated a side of me I'd never been privileged to see before. I did have value. I did have a purpose. For the first time in my life, I felt like I actually knew who I was. The shadows of depression and confusion began fading.

I walked away from that sacred experience with a pronounced, God-given mission for my existence. I share this mission openly and as a means of accountability with as many as will help hold me to it:

> **My mission in life is to bless my brothers and sisters,**
> **who are God's children, to live a higher**
> **level of spiritual strength.**
> **It is to influence as many as possible.**

Now, I am not here to defend or debate that divine directive. It's mine, it's not yours, nor do I believe it should be yours. You were planted in a different part of the world than I was, and in much different circumstances. Your soil is not mine. Our weather and seasonal patterns do not align. And yet we share one thing in common: we rely on water for life. We rely on a reason, a motive and a source to ground us.

What's yours?

If you have yet to discover a solid answer to that question, then I invite you to keep reading. If you *can* answer it, I may just challenge your answer.

Finding Water

"No water, no life. No blue, no green."
—Sylvia Earle

Have you ever had someone look you straight in the eyes and say something so profound, so moving, that it felt as if they had reached into your soul, pulled at your heart strings and realigned every part of your being? Chad Hymas did that for me, sitting from his wheelchair.

The *Wall Street Journal* has called Chad, "One of the ten most inspirational people in the world".[11] He is one of the youngest ever to be inducted into the National Speaker Hall of Fame. In 2001, at the age of twenty-seven, Chad's life changed in one traumatic moment when a 2,000-pound bale of hay shattered his neck, leaving him a quadriplegic. His life since that tragic day has been miraculous, to say the least.

Chad is the president of his own communications company and an Internet marketing company. He travels up to 300,000 miles a year, all around the world. He instills hope and personal transformation for professional and civic organizations at the highest level. In 2003, Chad set a world record by wheeling his chair from Salt Lake City to Las Vegas (513 miles). And amongst all of this, he finds some of his greatest joys at home with his wife and three children.

I had the privilege of being with Chad in a very intimate setting,

---

[11] https://www.wsj.com/articles/SB116070526962791503

sitting up front in a room of about forty people. I was attending a life mastery retreat for the weekend. The location was a serenely set club-house at a pristine golf course and resort. The striking green was quite the contrast to the beautiful red canyons of southern Utah.

Chad was the keynote speaker for this event. The theme for the retreat was *Vision*. He didn't disappoint.

There are two things I'll never forget about that time we had together. The first, I'm ashamed to say, is the curiosity, no, let's be honest, the doubt and skepticism I had about Chad. *What can a Hall of Fame speaker say that I haven't already heard?* was the egotistical question that parked in the backseat of my brain. Even as he started speaking, I sadly continued to carry some criticism and judgment as to his approach and delivery.

And then, in a moment I least expected, he caught me with his eyes and locked on. The whole world seemed to stop for a few brief seconds. "God wants you to live your purpose and passion. Don't know what your passion is? Go serve someone."

Sonic boom!

My mental sound barrier, the limiting beliefs I had been coddling up to that point during Chad's talk, had just been shattered by a few simple words with a nearly indescribable force behind them. And yet it wasn't the words themselves that were emphatically shaking my core as much as it was the meaning and feeling that accompanied them.

I bet you know what I'm talking about. I'm certain you've had your own defining moments in life that seem darn near impossible to explain to others; those emotions that stirred inside of you leave you changed forever, never able to go back to the way you were before. That's what Chad did to me.

I felt that not only had a vision been opened up to me about me, but that someone else was feeling and seeing me for the very first time. I was exposed. And it was wonderful and glorious and terrifying all at the same time.

I wrote down as quickly as I could what he had said and what I'd felt, though the tears welling up made it a bit challenging. I'm not sure what else Chad shared during the rest of that talk, as I was replaying over and over again what he'd left on the six-foot round table that stood between the two of us. My fingers caressed the lined paper of my small, leather notebook and each word kept jumping off the page.

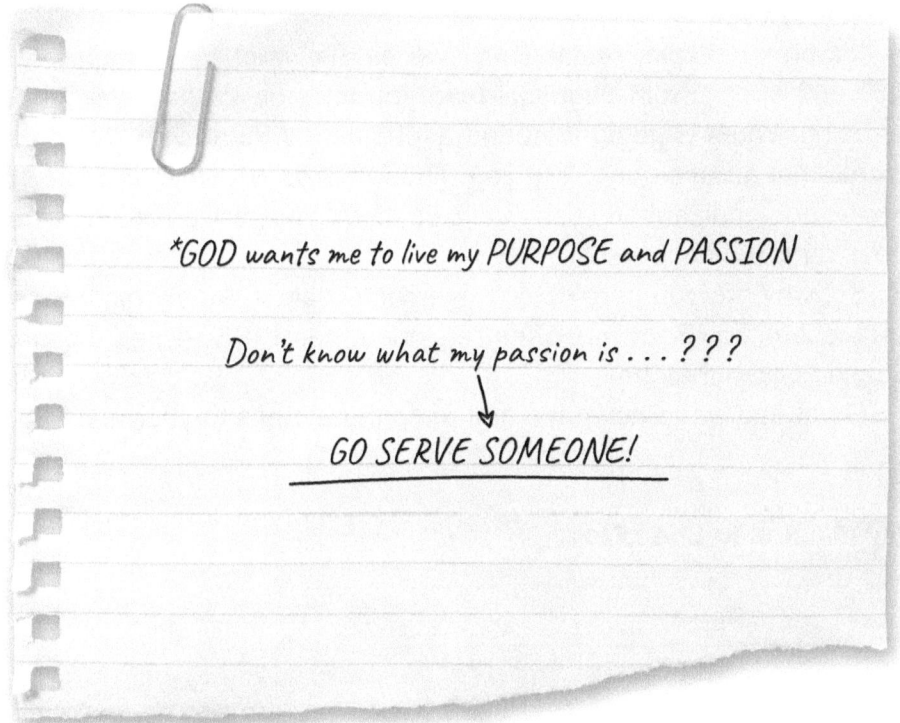

*GOD wants me to live my PURPOSE and PASSION

Don't know what my passion is . . . ? ? ?

GO SERVE SOMEONE!

Man! Even now, as I write those words on this page, their resounding impact lands just as powerfully as they did that day with Chad. It's different, though; this time around, there's an urgency and excitement to give this away rather than holding onto it for my own self-discovery.

I know precisely what those electrifying words have done for me and for countless others I've coached. And now, I pass them on to you. I want *you* to live your purpose and passion. I really have no idea what that might be. Maybe you don't either.

This I do know: If you forget yourself and go out and serve someone, you'll find it. It may not happen instantaneously. I can promise you that if you do this with enough consistency, with an open and selfless heart, you'll find it. And when you do, you'll know it.

One of Zig Ziglar's timeless sayings sums this up so well: "You can have everything in life you want, if you will just help other people get what they want."

It's pretty simple, really. Don't we all just want to be happy and fulfilled? Your Life Mission will lead you right up to that idyllic state of being. Yours is going to sound a lot different than mine. You'll use words that are meaningful to you. Those words will strike chords that are so personal, nobody can duplicate them. They will be as unique as your very own fingerprints.

So, why are you here? Don't overcomplicate it. As my ninth-grade art teacher, Mr. Goodwin, often reminded me, "KISS—Keep it simple stupid." I liked that guy!

Go ahead, write down the first thing that comes to your mind right now.

My Mission In Life is to...

_____

_____

_____

_____

_____

_____

You can refine this later if you'd like. Make it yours. Be sure to include words that move you and light you up inside.

It's a mission that, just like an oak's taproot, gets you to the source. Once there, your growth will become exponential. Your ability to reach out and up will be unlimited. Every decision you make, belief you hold onto and principle that guides you will be based on this mission.

Think about it as a mission to outer space: WE ARE GOING TO THE MOON! Should we bring the monkey? You tell me, does it help us get to the moon? What about painting the rocket ship pink? Ummm, does it help us get to the moon? Do we spend this money on this research or not? I don't know, you tell me. . .does it help us get to the moon!?

Listen, *you* are going to the moon! And you deserve to know what that looks like. So, please, take this seriously. Own this Life Mission as if your life depended on it. Because, frankly, it does.

CHAPTER THREE

Things Which Matter Most

"Your core values are the deeply held beliefs
that authentically describe your soul."
—John Maxwell

I remember walking into my older brother's house one day where I found him seated at the kitchen island doing some work on his laptop. There was an array of activity going on around him as his wife was getting dinner ready, and I sat back to take it all in for a moment. *Deep breaths, Andrew.* One child was singing and dancing while watching a music video on YouTube, and another was playing a video game on their TV. Another was laughing and squealing as she came down the slide from their castle (yes, a built-in castle in their upstairs bonus room), while another was plunking away on the piano. I'm sure the last of their five kids was doing something else that for some reason my brain just can't recall.

I looked at Adam in amazed wonder and asked, "How are you able to get any work done around here?"

He looked up and said, "What?" He didn't even know I was there or that there were any potential distractions around him.

"How can you concentrate with all this noise?"

I was shocked at his response. "Oh, I love it! It fuels me. Sometimes I'd just rather be out here than in my office."

Fun, energy, excitement, laughter, play—these are some of my brother's values, but mostly *fun*. On the flip side, one day, his four-year-old son walked into *my* home, stopped, took a look around and said, "It feels like a temple in here!"

Peace, order, calmness, serenity—these are some of my values. I'm sure you can see how well my brother and I complement one another.

Lateral Roots:

> *"In matters of style, swim with the current; in*
> *matters of principle, stand like a rock."*
> *—Thomas Jefferson*

Values and principles. Principles and values. These two ideas are thrown around a lot these days, whether in a boardroom, an entrepreneurial launch or family meetings. It seems like as soon as something trendy gains traction and starts sticking, it can often and quickly lose its power, becoming diluted and soon forgotten. I fear this might be the case when it comes to principles and values. Let's not let this happen in our personal lives.

Think of it like this: If our Life Mission, the taproot, is derived from the source and gives us meaning, drive and a grounding motive, then our values and principles are the lateral roots that expand outward, creating a stable foundation for continual growth in all aspects of our life.

If our Life Mission is the WHY, literally answering the question, *Why am I here?* our principles and values, then, are the HOW, *How am I going to live my life and bring forth this mission?* And the WHAT? We'll get to that later, mark my words.

IDENTIFYING VALUES

Values are fascinating. They co-exist with and are directly connected to our Life Mission. They help to describe what's most important in our lives. Just like the lateral roots of an oak tree that grow out of the taproot, our values are derived from and grow out of our mission.

My brother values fun because part of his life's mission is to squeeze every possible ounce out of everything life has to offer. This makes it easy for him to decide whether they stay a few more days in Hawaii on a family vacation or go home as originally planned for the kids to get back to school.

Hidden beneath the surface of every great oak tree is a vast spread of powerful roots running horizontally four to seven times the width of its foliage. And just because you can't see them, doesn't mean they're not there. So it is with values—they exist, whether we're aware of them or not. When we're not aware of them, we find ourselves living a dull existence, void of fulfillment, always questioning, "What's wrong?"

The great writer and philosopher, Ayn Rand, said, "Happiness is that state of consciousness which proceeds from the achievement of one's values."[12] What this means then, is that our degree of happiness is in direct proportion to our knowledge of and commitment to our most deeply held values. Having clarity on your values is like knowing where your kids are; it puts your mind at ease. And certainly not knowing is *not* okay.

How do we identify these values? Well, you can spend hundreds and even thousands of dollars through quick, online assessments all the way up to weekend getaways and extended soul-searching retreats into the middle of nowhere. They all accomplish the same thing and can actually be done fairly quickly.

Let's look at an area of life we all have in common, one that some of us ignore, and none of us can run away from: Physical Fitness and Nutrition.

When it comes to Physical Fitness and Nutrition values, goals, and the likes, most people are all over the board. They don't actually know what they want and therefore never seem to be satisfied. They chase new and popular diets, workout routines, meal planning, intermittent fasting, not eating meat, only eating meat, fruit is bad for you, eat as much fruit as you like, and on and on and on. I believe this is because most of us do not sincerely have clarity on what we value in this area of life or how it ties to a Life Mission.

Let me give you an example. A few years back some colleagues and I were sitting in a circle, on the hard rubber mats of a kickboxing gym. It was December and we were on our yearly retreat, getting

---

[12] Ayn Rand (1988). "The Ayn Rand Lexicon: Objectivism from A to Z", p.213, Penguin

ready to refocus our goals and intentions for the next year. This was a fun way to get out of the confines of the office and bond.

The twenty-something-year-old instructor had each of us share a fitness goal we had been working on. When it came to me, I said, "I don't have any." You should have seen the bewildered faces of disbelief. I was the *only* coach in our office. And I didn't have any goals! You would have thought I had committed some outrageous crime against humanity or an unpardonable sin. Now, no one was actually pointing fingers or calling me out as a hypocrite, but I felt their condemnation, or at the very least, confusion.

I got on my next call with *my* coach and shared what had happened. I expressed a bit of shame around not having goals in this area of my life. He then taught me something I'll never forget.

He asked, "Andrew, what do you want when it comes to your physical fitness?"

I said, "To be able to run around and play with my kids, go skiing and mountain biking and hiking a couple times each year. Oh, and make sure my wife is still attracted to me. That's about it."

"Is that all happening for you right now?" he asked.

"Well, yeah, I guess," I answered.

"Then what do you need goals and workout routines and eating plans for? You're exactly where you want to be!"

I hadn't thought of it that way. I was habitually eating healthy. I was walking consistently, which allowed me to play with my kids and go adventure in the outdoors when I felt like it. And my wife (pretty sure she was being honest) said I was the perfect man (for her, at least). My coach was right: I was exactly where I wanted to be.

So, my values in that area of my life could have been summarized simply as:

- Playing with my kids
- Occasional outdoor sports
- Wife's approval

My values were not:

- Bigger muscles than most
- Able to run marathons
- 6% body fat

Now, if those *are* your values, that's great! They're not mine, though. Your values are unique to you and there's no judgment around them. Remember, values help us stay in alignment with our Life Mission. So, if my Life Mission was, "To drive myself to the upper limits of my physical capabilities, knowing, when all is said and done, that I did everything in my power to maximize this God-given body for all its worth," then my values might look like that guy back there with 6% body fat.

Once our values are aligned with our Life Mission, then we feel peace, fulfillment and a sense of accomplishment. If not, we get down on ourselves or maybe a bit anxious. We feel like there's more or maybe we start pointing fingers at ourselves or others, playing the blame game, which, by the way, no one ever wins, definitely a lose-lose endeavor.

Once you've got your Life Mission, now very simply, consider how your Physical Fitness and Nutrition play into that. Ponder this: In order to achieve my Mission in Life, what's important in the area of Physical Fitness and Nutrition?

Jot down what words come to mind, right here, right now.

_____   _____

_____   _____

_____   _____

_____   _____

How do you know when you've got them all? When you start repeat Go deeper, ask, what else is important to me?

_____   _____

_____   _____

_____   _____

_____   _____

How do you know when you've got them all? When you start repeat One more time, what else? There's no right or wrong number. I've seen anywhere from three values all the way up to twenty plus!

_____   _____

_____   _____

_____   _____

_____   _____

How do you know when you've got them all? When you start repeating words and you aren't able to come up with new ones, you'll know your list is complete. If you feel stuck and you know there's more, try this:

Think of a time in your life when you were totally motivated in the area of Physical Fitness and Nutrition. Can you think of a specific time? Go back to that moment. Close your eyes. Imagine you're there, in your own shoes, looking around. Take it all in. . .the sights, sounds, smells and temperature. What was the last thing you felt just before you were totally motivated? Can you give me a name for that feeling?

That emotion, right there, is a value. When I feel _____ I'm motivated in this area of my life.

Now, do that same memory jogger activity again. Remember, when you repeat a word on your list, you'll know you're done.

Just to make sure you're truly complete, ask this question: *With all of these values being present for me, is there anything that could happen that would make me not feel okay about this area of my life?* For example, I might answer that question with, *Well, if I have a heart attack I wouldn't be too happy with my Physical Fitness and Nutrition.* That means we'd need to add something like "Longevity" to my values list, or "Healthy Heart."

Go ahead and ask it again. Make sure to include the added value (like Longevity or Healthy Heart). If something pops up, then add it to your values list. If not, then you're golden.

Here's the last step. Take a look at those values and determine which is most important to you. What's your number one value in that area of life? What's next? Put them in order. Now, you've got your values prioritized. This kind of clarity emboldens us to make decisions from a place of true motivation, rather than giving in to all the other distracting influences that can easily sway us off course. It's so simple and enlightening to run a difficult choice that has to be made through your top values and, as a result, know what it is you really want. Try it. See what happens.

My Top Physical Fitness and Nutrition Values:

1) _____

2) _____

3) _____

4) _____

5) _____

Journal Entry ✎ What could this clarity on your values mean for how you'll choose to take care of your physical health moving forward? How might you make some changes in your fitness and nutrition routines based on this new understanding? What goals could you set for your-self given these newly discovered, motivating values?

CHAPTER FOUR

An Aim Worth Having

"Nothing is given to man on Earth - struggle is built into the nature of life…the hero is the man who lets no obstacle prevent him from pursuing the values he has chosen."
—Andrew Bernstein

I've found that defining our values and then explaining them to others can be tricky. Take "integrity" for example. You and I and everyone else on this planet probably have a slightly different internal representation for what integrity means. For you it might mean that you always do what you say, down to every detail. You say you'll be there at 3:00 p.m. and you show up at 3:04 p.m. and now you consider yourself to be out of integrity. For someone else it may be less precise and more of a measure of moral character and commitment to principles.

Understanding what your values are is the first vital step. Being able to define, communicate and help others understand them is the next. If not, we're just throwing perfectly good seeds on top of concrete with a wish and prayer that somehow something good's going to come from it.[13]

DEFINING VALUES

Here's a simple activity to help you define your values. You may not do this for each and every one of your values, but if you have more than five, you'll certainly want to do it for the first five.

---

[13] Special thanks to Dr. Matt James and the Empowerment Partnership for teaching me these powerful skills around values.

Let's run "integrity" through this example and pretend like we're talking about another area of life; instead, let's no longer use Physical Fitness and Nutrition, but Relationships/Significant Other.

Here's an example of how someone might answer these:

- How do you know when you're experiencing *integrity* in your relationship? ....not experiencing *integrity*?
  1. When my partner and I have agreed upon expectations and they're being met.
  2. When I or my partner does something that goes against what we agreed on.
- What does that (whatever you wrote for each of those) mean to you?
  1. It means that I can trust my partner and he/she can trust me as well and that makes me feel safe.
  2. It means that I don't know if I can trust my partner and that creates some fears.
- How do you know when someone is helping you be *in integrity*? .... Is not helping you be *in integrity*?
  1. When my partner is holding me accountable to what I've promised.
  2. When he/she lets me off the hook and doesn't call me out.
- What is your evidence procedure for feeling *in integrity*? (How do you know when you've got it?) ....not feeling *in integrity*? (How do you know when you don't have it?)
  1. When we don't question each other's actions and things are smooth.
  2. When we argue about who said or did something that went against perceived expectations.
- What causes you to feel *in integrity*? ....not feel *in integrity*?
  1. When I feel trusted, able to trust my partner, and we are connected.
  2. When that trust is lacking or when there seems to be some-thing keeping us from being close.

So, again, the questions are:

- *How do you know when you're _____ (insert value)? ....not _____?*
  1.
  2.
- *What does that mean to you? (Go deeper on what you wrote for 1 and 2 above.)*
  1.
  2.
- *How do you know when someone is helping you be _____? .... is not helping you be _____?*
  1.
  2.
- *What is your evidence procedure for feeling _____? (How do you know when you've got it?) ....not feeling _____? (How do you know when you don't have it?)*
  1.
  2.
- *What causes you to feel _____? ....not feel _____?*
  1.
  2.

Being able to put thoughts and words toward your values allows you to grasp them even better. You can literally hand these definitions over to a significant other, friend, coworker or family member and connect in an intimate way that you may have never been able to in times past.

This ability to really know your values, communicate them and empower others to support you is like a secret weapon. You are sharing something that no one might have known before. You are giving away a key to unlock a power that has maybe never been tapped into. Think about what could happen when all of those values are unlocked.

THE WHEEL OF LIFE

What if a tree had only one lateral root? Absurd, right? Yeah, but what if that root was the biggest, strongest, most nutrient absorbing, water-sucking root that ever existed? That doesn't matter. Think about a piano. The most beautiful key that plays your favorite note cannot create a masterpiece without including the other eighty-seven keys. So, you may play that integrity note better than anyone in the world, and yet if you're neglecting other values, you're missing out on some incredible, bottled-up potential for happiness.

The first time I did the Wheel of Life exercise I was all over the place, some high numbers, some low numbers and some pretty mediocre numbers. There was nothing impressive or robust about its shape or size. It helped me gain awareness and find focus for that which deserved the most attention for my personal progress.

Each area of our life carries different values. Some may overlap and some may be very unique.

Consider these six areas in your Wheel of Life:

THE WHEEL OF LIFE

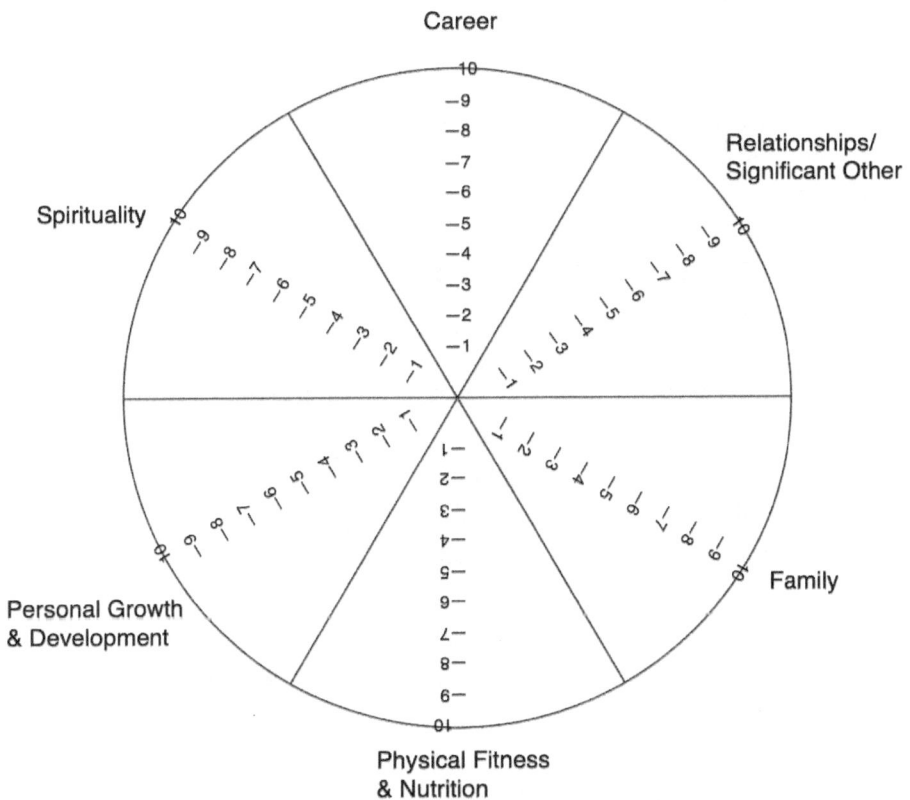

The numbers represent fulfillment. A "ten" means you are highly fulfilled in that area. It doesn't necessarily mean that you've accomplished everything you've ever wanted to or hit every single goal you've set, but it does mean that you're feeling pretty good with where you're at. If you were to die today, there'd be no regrets. It doesn't mean everything's perfect, but you're happy with where you're at in that area. We are comparing you to where you *desire* to be today rather than where you *could* be tomorrow.

A "one" means you're at the end of your rope. There's not a lot of hope. The light at the end of the tunnel is almost imperceptible. You're ready to throw in the towel.

Go ahead and do a quick assessment as to how fulfilled you are in each area. Be honest.

Career _____ / 10
Relationship/Significant Other _____ / 10
Family _____ / 10
Physical Fitness & Nutrition _____ / 10
Personal Growth & Development _____ / 10
Spirituality _____ / 10

When we are struggling in a certain area, it means we either don't have clarity on what our values are in that part of our life, or we're not truly living up to them. You may consider pausing at this point and going through and identifying what your values are for each of the six areas. Or maybe you bookmark this page and come back to it later. It's up to you.

And, you may choose not to, and if so, no judgment. But please, take a second to read and reread this telling observation from Henry Seidel Canby:[14]

"Millions...fritter away their lives ...They live fast, but neither hard nor deep. They live too fast because they don't know where they are going, and so have to hurry to get there...These millions have never stopped long enough to calculate what is an aim worth having. They really don't know what they want."

I'm going to invite you to slow down here. Can you go hard for a moment? Are you willing to get off the surface level and go deep on this? You choose. And before you make that choice, take another look

---

[14] I transcribed this from Earl Nightingale's "The Essence of Success" audio book

at your wheel. Is it round? I've seen some pretty awesome shapes as I've done this with clients over the years: triangles, lima beans, shapes that would certainly have you scratching your head if you were to see them attached to any kind of vehicle.

Is your wheel big or small? How confident would you feel about your wheel's capacity to travel at high speeds down the freeway? Would it be a rocky ride? Maybe your wheel is barely hanging on with one measly, crooked, rusty old bolt, waiting for life's next pothole to send it tumbling through rush hour traffic. Are you looking at this Wheel of Life wondering how it got so bent out of shape? What areas would you say need to be pumped up with a bit of air, infused with some TLC?

Whether yours is looking like it needs a complete resurrection from the junkyard or just a simple tune up, it's time to own your outcomes. This is the one and only life you've been gifted. Let's take care of this gift by knowing, inside and out, what it's capable of and how we can get the absolute most mileage possible. Nobody likes being stranded on the side of the road, waiting for a friend, AAA or having to change your own spare tire.

This can be a sobering experience, taking extreme accountability for where you're really at in your life. Here's some hope. It's a story of a client we'll call Ben.

Ben had gone through the ringer. When we started working together, his wheel was depleted of almost all air. No one knew the demons he was battling on a daily basis. He'd been hiding behind a charismatic personality and a selfless habit of service to others. But, on the inside, and behind the scenes, he felt like he'd failed his family and his Creator. Ben was all kinds of broken and scared.

As I carefully worked with and enabled him to let go of long-seeded, unconscious decisions, self-deprecating beliefs and detrimental emotions, Ben came back to life! He quickly caught a glimpse of what a ten out of ten could look like in each individual area on his Wheel of Life. As we moved forward, together, creating new goals and dreams that would take him to places of unprecedented purpose and fulfillment, Ben beamed with a newness of joy. His wife thanked me in the sincerest way for the impact of his transformation on their marriage and family.

I'll always be grateful for my final coaching session with Ben. After a year of working together, we filled out a new Wheel of Life to compare where he now stood to where he was when we started. As I asked, "On a scale from one to ten, how fulfilled are you in this area of your life?" he confidently and tearfully, with a genuine and joyful smile, answered, "Ten." It wasn't just for one aspect of his wheel, he repeated, "Ten. Ten. Ten..." for each area of his life.

No matter what your wheel looks like, there's hope, I assure you. We just need to stop for a bit and do some work. And it's far better to prepare and prevent now than to repair and repent later. Let's be proactive. Here we go.

Journal Entry 🖉 *What insights are you having as you look at your Wheel of Life? What emotions are coming up for you? If you could pick just one area that you'd like to focus on for the remainder of your reading of this book, which one would you choose? What would a "ten" look like, sound like, feel like for you in this area in one year from now?*

The Area I Choose to Focus on in my Life Right Now is:

_____

CHAPTER FIVE

Until One Is Committed

*"There are only two options regarding commitment; you're
either in or you're out. There's no such thing as life in-between."*
—*Pat Riley*

Each Memorial Day, for as long as I can remember, I've joined my mom and dad in gathering flowers from our neighbors' yards (yes, buying them would not be the frugal thing to do) and visiting our ancestors' graves, paying tribute to the pioneered paths they paved for the abundant life we now enjoy. As I pause at each one, pushing back blades of neatly mowed, dead grass, my mind considers the impressionable legacy left by each one. And I can't help but wonder, *What will my legacy be?* Have you ever really thought about yours? How will you be remembered by those who will walk the paths you've pioneered?

If I were to ever have the honor of choosing an epitaph for the future headstone of John van der Giessen, it would say "Larger Than Life." As cliché and oft repeated as it might sound, there are no better words to describe this mountain of a man.

At the time of this writing, I have now known John for more than eight years. For over seven of those years, I've had the unique privilege of personally coaching him in his life and business. My respect and admiration for John runs as pure as gold. He has become a trusted brother and endeared friend, and I'll tell you why: his devotion to his values is just as strong if not stronger than any muscle on his sturdy frame.

John laughs that his first driver's license listed him at a mere 125 pounds and 5'7" (sopping wet and on his tippy toes). On top of that, he was severely asthmatic and allergic to pretty much everything, not the best scenario for growing up in rural Idaho where an overabundance of animals and farming surrounded him constantly. While he enjoyed playing recreational sports as a youngster, he never thought about competing at a higher level to any extent. He certainly didn't possess great skills, talents or desires to master any athletic pursuit.

At eighteen, John found himself at the University of Idaho with no plans and little direction. In high school, he'd been an average student at best and kept that trend right into his freshman year of college where he barely managed to pull a 1.7 GPA (passing by the skin of his teeth with a C- average). He stuck around for another year, and in the fall of 2001, a fellow fraternity brother invited him out to play in the University of Idaho's Twenty-fifth Anniversary Rugby Reunion Tournament. John had no idea what rugby was. He'd never even heard the word "rugby" before! But, for the heck of it, he showed up to play and enjoyed breaking a bunch of unknown rugby rules and getting banged up a bit. He had a blast! Saying 'yes' to that opportunity sent him down a path of curiosity.

He went to the library and did a quick Internet search. John discovered that the Rugby World Cup would be held in Australia in 2003. Something stirred inside him and he found himself applying for a study abroad program at The University of Queensland, hoping to be able to watch some rugby while working toward his college degree. To his chagrin, he was denied admittance based on his low grade-point average. Undaunted, he called the school's admissions' office and was told he needed to go down there in person if he wanted to appeal the decision.

So, in the spring of 2003, with a mom willing to take out a private loan and invest in her son, John purchased a one-way ticket to Sydney and flew away with a driving desire that couldn't be quenched. I asked John what motivated him to make such a big decision with so little assurance of any particular outcome. His answer, "Freedom to find myself with zero limitations or excuses. Freedom to say 'yes' and to explore and to grow."

Freedom…John's number one value in life.

This unyielding commitment to freedom led John down an eight-year path of collegiate, professional and international rugby competition. In 2011, John flew to New Zealand with the US National Team, playing amongst the greatest in the world. They ended up beating Russia in that tournament, a feat very few can say they have ever achieved. John summed up that victory in one word, "Amazing!"

In total, John was selected to play in nineteen international matches, when many players only get to play in one such game their entire career. He was appointed the honor of Captain, and played professionally up until the last pool match versus Italy in the 2011 Rugby World Cup.

You see, John gets it. When it comes to commitment to values, he's all in. It's a "burn the boats" mentality. One-way ticket. No turning back. **Strength of the Oak**.

What about you? Are you willing to light that match, toss it into the past and never look back? Can you look at yourself in the mirror at this precise moment and say, "Listen, here are the values in my life that matter most. Today I choose to take a stand with bold conviction in my heart. I am locked and loaded, moving forward in a pursuit of courage. No longer will I wait for permission from an unknown source. I'm all in on my values."

If you're not that committed, what are you holding on to that makes it so heavy and hard to move forward? What are your excuses? What's the self-limiting chatter that unconsciously repeats over and over and over again inside your head? What emotions aren't serving you and need to be dealt with now? If you've come this far into the book and you're not ready, willing or able to play full out with your Life Mission and values, then we need to pause a moment.

Why not? What's holding you back? What's the block all about? Get real on this with me, would you please? Write down what you're thinking and feeling here. Acknowledge where you're at. We'll circle back around to this later. I just need you to see it and keep it in your sights.

If you're still reading, it means you can look yourself in the mirror with 100% conviction, knowing that you're strapped in and we're taking this rocket to the moon...ready or not! If not, then I implore you to commit, take action, make up your mind, be all in!

To me, this is what "all in" looks like. Below I share my interpretation of W. H. Murray's moving words from The Scottish Himalayan Expedition:

"Until one is committed,
there is hesitancy, the chance to draw back..."

When it comes to our initiatives and desires to create, we all too often omit a fundamental truth. In doing so, we end up killing off the grandest of plans. And what's that truth?

"that the moment one definitely commits oneself,
then Providence moves too.
All sorts of things occur to help one
that would otherwise never have occurred."

From that decision to be all in, all kinds of happenings begin to stream into being. Unthought of resources, people, financial assistance, almost seemingly impossible miracles come forth. Murray goes on to share his utmost respect for the mantra attributed to Goethe:

"Whatever you can do, or dream you can...begin it.
Boldness has genius, power, and magic in it.
Begin it now!"

When this quote first fell in my lap, it landed like a load of bricks. I was recently divorced and living alone for the first time in forever. The loneliness was killing me, trying to figure out what to do in the evenings when there was no longer family dinner, little girl bedtime routines, household chores or connecting as a couple when everything finally settled down.

On top of the loneliness, I was navigating a complex co-parenting plan that didn't seem to make any sense. I felt like my manhood was being ruthlessly ripped out of my heart. *Why should I have to fight to spend time with my daughters? Is this what being a dad is going to look like now? This sucks!*

I was grinding through each day, prospecting for clients that I could serve in real estate, knocking on doors, holding open houses, making phone calls and attending as many classes as possible. I had sales in the pipeline, but my meager savings from being a teacher was slowly dwindling and the rate of replenishment was not sufficient. A defeated thought entered. *Maybe this isn't right for me. What if I fail my way out of the business? I don't know if I'm going to be able to provide for myself and my family. What will people think?*

I was at the end of my rope. Then I looked up.

Check out this journal entry dated November 22, 2014:

> I can change how I react to all of this. I can put my trust in God and not allow the actions of others to determine the outcome of my life. My faith in and relationship with my Heavenly Father, my willingness to be grateful and find joy in life, my relationship with my girls and those I love most, and ultimately my attitude is up to me and no one else. I can do this. One step is enough for me. Take ye therefore no thought for the morrow. I can do today. I don't know about tomorrow. All I know is...I can do today.

"The moment one definitely commits oneself, then Providence moves too." I was committed. I had to have faith that Providence was moving. The boldness, genius, power and magic in my dream was to rebuild me, my ability to love again, to be the father I knew I could be and to live out my Life Mission with every curveball that was coming my way. This is what I learned *All In* means to me. Like turning the tips of your skis right into that powdery descent, shifting your weight forward, there's only one way to go from here. No turning back.

And I didn't. Providence did move. Powerfully.

With a Life Mission in hand—your own personal constitution—and clarity of values to go along with it, you are well on your way to building a solid, unwavering foundation for your life.

While your Life Mission and values are highly personal, private and totally subjective to you, principles are public and proven, universal laws that objectively guide the world we live in. Put them together, and you can achieve anything. I agree with Edison, "If we did all the things we are capable of doing, we would literally astound ourselves."[15]

Let's dig a bit deeper on principles.

PRINCIPLES

> *"Many men do not allow their principles to take root, but*
> *pull them up every now and then, as children do the*
> *flowers they have planted, to see if they are growing."*
> —*Henry Wadsworth Longfellow*

Don't you love that quote by Longfellow? The image of a small child pulling up that flower just brings a smile to my face—so innocent and shamelessly naive all at the same time.

A principle is just as sure and steadfast as that flower's future, at least if not pulled up by the roots. You can take it to the bank and cash it in anytime. Principles are truths, universal in nature. And just like laws of nature, they're not going anywhere or changing anytime soon. Here are some quick examples:

- *What goes up, must come down (law of nature).*
- *When you tell the truth, people can trust you (principle).*

---

[15] Motivating Humans: Goals, Emotions, and Personal Agency Beliefs (1992) by Martin E. Ford, p. 17.

We do not control laws of nature just as we do not control universal principles. If we try to ignore them or pretend to not believe in them, they don't just disappear. This means we have a choice: Will we work *with* them or continue to avoid, gnash our teeth in resistance or complain about them?

How well has complaining about laws of nature, like gravity or the weather, ever worked for anyone? I'm sure no farmer has ever complained about the rain falling *down* and not the other way around. I've never heard a surfer whine about the sun being too bright and the waves too big because of the distance between the sun, the moon and the earth?

Like the farmer and surfer, we too can identify what these natural laws, life principles are and how to use them for our benefit and enjoyment.

GROUNDED TO GROWING UP

Let's explore some basic ways that we can identify, learn and live by guiding life principles.

An influential leader was once asked how he was able to get so many people to follow him. Very simply he stated, "I teach them correct principles and they govern themselves." The world's greatest leaders are driven by principles. They live those principles and allow others the opportunity to likewise live them or leave them.

As we look to the pioneering leaders of business, religion, philosophy and philanthropy, we find common threads running among all of them. These threads are success principles. As motivational philosopher Brian Tracy so aptly put it, "Life is like a combination lock; your job is to find the right numbers, in the right order, so you can have anything you want." Principles are the numbers in that combination that unlock your power and potential.

Here's a quick story that helped me define a few principles at a critical time in my life.

Remember that guy I told you about who was thirty years old, divorced, and living in his parents' basement? Me! I had just left a six-year teaching career and went into a 100% commission-based, independent-contractor, sales career—real estate. I had no clue just how much mental fortitude, emotional tenacity and social stamina it would take to succeed. No licensing classes would adequately prepare me for what was to come.

I can recall, vividly, the exact location when the following phone call took place. I was first sitting and then pacing around a circular glass table in a small conference room of the real estate brokerage I'd recently joined. A dearly admired and much respected mentor and family member said to me, "Andrew, I'm worried about this career choice. Seems to me that the most successful real estate agents that I know are women in their fifties. I just don't want to see you fail. How are you going to be able to provide for your family?"

I couldn't believe what I was hearing! It felt like he'd just swung a pillowcase full of bricks right into my stomach.

My reply? "You know, I appreciate your concern... *and* the Realtor of the Year this past year was a thirty-two-year-old guy with a young family. If he can do it, so can I."

I don't remember anything else about that conversation except for the wildfire it lit directly and instantaneously beneath me. He didn't quite understand what my wife has come to learn about me, with what she might call extreme clarity, "If you want to get Andrew to do something, just tell him he can't." She even had a custom canvas painted with the words, *We Don't Say Can't – Andrew L. Anderson* staring you right in the face as you enter our kitchen.

The fire that was set ablaze by that unsolicited phone call created an insatiable hunger in me. I wanted to know what every successful agent was doing, reading, what classes they were going to, the trainings and conferences they attended and what they ate for lunch! I knew that success left clues and I was willing to sniff them out.

I didn't exactly know it at the time, and yet as I look back, with 20/20 hindsight, I now realize that I was identifying, learning and striving to internalize significant principles of success. Here are my top five success principles, those that I have clung onto and therefore, have had the greatest impact on me throughout the years.

My Top 5 Success Principles

1. **"There is no chance, no destiny, no fate that can circumvent, hinder or control the firm resolve of a determined soul." –Ella Wheeler Wilcox**[16]
2. **Your cells eavesdrop on your thoughts.**
3. **Change the way you look at things and the things you look at change.**[17]
4. **"The cave you fear to enter holds the treasure you seek." –Joseph Campbell**[18]
5. **Everyone is doing the best they can with the resources they have available.**[19]

These are the rules I learned to follow, my guiding life principles. What are yours?

I invite you to take some time and make your five, six, or seven principles for success. Maybe you've got a Top Ten list. You definitely don't need one hundred, although you might have that many or more. You could also look back on journal entries from your past, if you have them. Think back to times in your life when you were the most fulfilled, productive, in flow, successful and happy. What rules were you playing by? Whose rules were you playing by?

Ask those who know you best—family members, friends, colleagues, clients. Be vulnerable, humble and pose it this way, "Hey, I'm

---

[16] Ella Wheeler Wilcox (2012). "Leafs On An Idle Breeze - My Inspirational Poems (Annotated Edition)", p.497, Jazzybee Verlag
[17] BOLD Laws from kwMAPS Coaching
[18] 2004, Conscious Courage: Turning Everyday Challenges Into Opportunities by Maureen Stearns, Quote Page 15, Enrichment Books, Seminole, Florida. (Google Books Preview) https://quoteinvestigator.com/2013/05/23/campbell-treasure/
[19] The Empowerment Partnership's NLP Training.

on a quest to really get grounded and rooted in my life. I'm defining life principles for my success. What do you see as the rules I live by when I'm at my best? What are yours?"

What about those you look up to most in your life? You might take a second to write down their names. Start with three to five, maybe there's nine or ten. What is it about these people that you admire most? Certainly, they have qualities and values you wish to emulate, and yet, what we're looking for here are *principles*, the guiding truths they implement to have the influence you desire to have as well.

As you carefully build this list, you're setting up the framework to support endless possibilities of growth. The eighteenth century Irish writer, Phillip Skelton, said, "Our principles are the springs of our actions; our actions, the springs of our happiness or misery. Too much care, therefore, cannot be taken in forming our principles."[20]

I know it might seem tempting to just keep flying through the book at surface level. And to be honest, I don't want you to "just get through" the book. What I want is for this book to get through *you*. These ideas may save your life, or at least prevent you from living one that's small, boring, mediocre at best, which is actually killing off your potential!

Please, get this list together. Make it your personal playbook for success. Don't let a day go by without knowing how you're going to show up.

---

[20] This is the electronic version on Google Books, pp. 434-435
https://play.google.com/books/reader?id=jOYGAAAAQAAJ&pg=GBS.PA434&hl=en

MY PERSONAL PLAYBOOK FOR SUCCESS:
GUIDING LIFE PRINCIPLES

CHAPTER SIX

Stress Wood: Tried and Tested

*"He that always gives way to others will end
in having no principles of his own."*
—Aesop

After seven years of planning and construction and $150 million, "The Project that Will Save the World," *Biosphere 2*, was ready to go. In the fall of 1991, eight scientist-explorers were sealed into an airtight, three acre, mini-world located in southern Arizona. The goal was to spend two years studying how a mini-biosphere of ocean, wilderness, farms, animals and humans would work with as few outside influences as possible.

As you might imagine, several scientific insights and discoveries were made inside this closed ecological system, one of which surprisingly unveiled the effect of wind on trees.

The trees inside this man-made mini-world grew at an accelerated rate and yet never reached full maturity before losing branches and inevitably falling over. In nature, trees are exposed to wind. And wind was something they hadn't planned for inside the biosphere. Without wind, these trees never developed what is known as "stress wood."[21]

So, what is stress wood? Think of the swaying and movement of the leaves and branches resulting from wind. This movement places stress on the load-bearing components of the tree. The result is stress wood, the wood that is grown to compensate and make the tree stronger. This stress on the tree creates a vital environment for it to mature appropriately.

Douglas Malloch penned these touching words:

---

[21] https://dartmouthalumnimagazine.com/articles/biosphere-2-what-really-happened

Good timber does not grow with ease,
The stronger wind, the stronger trees,
The further sky, the greater length,
The more the storm, the more the strength.
By sun and cold, by rain and snow,
In trees and men good timbers grow.[22]

Just as a thriving tree has well-established stress wood, our principles also must be tried, tested and proven. Principles are everlastingly true *only* if and when they stand the test of time. As we experience the winds of life, we must never give way; rather, we must hold fast to our roots. Though painful at times, we cannot curse the stress or the time that it takes to solidify these principles—principles that allow for a lifetime of unlimited growth.

Personally, I think that patience is one of the hardest principles that must be followed regularly in our lives. For example, think about a proficient potter who knows to never hurry the burning, baking and drying process of the fiery kiln. This gentle artist trusts the work of her own hands along with the imperative means of transforming the wet clay into a solid masterpiece. She knows that sometimes it is in the waiting rather than the completing that we grow the most. Her willing patience is the price that must be paid, the principle that she adheres to. And the reward for patience? More patience! It's a surefire investment, every time. Patience is the selfish gift we give to ourselves that keeps on giving.

Once the debt of time and experience has been lifted, there is total and complete ownership of the principle. It's yours. The whirlwinds of life have blown and blasted, the critics have howled and hammered and while leaves and limbs may be strewn chaotically across the ground, the dependability of the roots has been confirmed. The principles are in place. Stress wood is present. And with a sturdy trunk, growth is now almost guaranteed. **Strength of the Oak**.

---

[22] Malloch, Douglas. "Good Timber," The Journal of Education 95, no. 6 (February 9, 1922): 146.

Journal Entry ✎ *When have you personally experienced a trying time that produced much needed stress wood strength for where you are today? What did you learn about your own character from that hardship? What do you see in your life right now that will require you to show up similarly or even better? What strength are you seeing develop deep within you during this time?*

> "Important principles may, and must, be inflexible."
> —Abraham Lincoln

It takes faith, an unbending trust in our roots, to ensure that we can withstand the storm. We must choose to bring an undeterred reliance to our Life Mission and values. Holding firmly to these convictions is the life source for the formation of lifelong success principles.

Show me a man who knows WHY he's here (Mission), a man who has absolute clarity on HOW he'll live his life to manifest this mission (values and principles), and I'll show you a man who can do WHATever his imagination and volition desire.

Nehemiah was such a man. Never heard of him? Buckle up, this is going to be a great ride!

I CANNOT COME DOWN

Let's take a look back to 444 BC, Jerusalem. Yes, that's a *long* time ago. And while I wasn't there personally, I've read and taught countless times about what was going on back then. I am fascinated by the story of an unlikely hero.

The desperate and despondent nation of Israel was looking for answers, comfort, something, anything to put their minds at ease. They had been conquered by the Persian Empire and were not allowed to rebuild their temple, the sacred place of worship that represented God's presence.

Upon hearing of the distressed condition of the Jews, Nehemiah, cupbearer to the king of Persia, could not hide the deep grief he felt for his people. A stroke of mercy fell upon the king as he granted Nehemiah permission to return to his homeland so that restoration could begin.

The builders were met with intense opposition. Neighboring nations mocked and sought to thwart Nehemiah and his fellow Jews from accomplishing so great a work. Fearless and focused, he proceeded as planned, organizing his resources and people to move forward in rebuilding the City of David.

Nehemiah's enemies continued to conspire, even threatening to attack. The aforementioned fearlessness was fading fast as the dangers of invasion became more and more real to the Jews. It was, to say the least, a very tense time as every worker "had his sword girded by his side, and so builded" (Nehemiah 4:18). Can you imagine rebuilding the walls of one of the greatest cities on Earth while holding onto your sword? These were scary times.

Seeing the progress, Nehemiah's enemies became ever more desperate. In four different attempts, they petitioned him to leave the safety of the city and meet with them, professing a desire to bring resolution to this conflict. Not to be deceived by their plot, each time Nehemiah countered their requests with the same resolute answer, "I am doing a great work, so that I cannot come down" (Nehemiah 6:3).

What a response! Is there a single word that can sum up Nehemiah's extraordinary attitude and character? You decide:

Grit. Determination. Resolve. Undeterred. Relentless. Bold. Tenacity. Decisive. Conviction. Dedication. Fortitude. Backbone. Adamant. Valor. Indomitable. Heart. Drive. Guts. Dauntless.

With such an unshakeable purpose of heart and mind, the walls of Jerusalem were rebuilt in an astounding fifty-two days. He never did succumb to the snares of his bloodthirsty detractors. Nehemiah the cupbearer, protector of the king, now became Nehemiah the governor, protector of all Israel. **Strength of the Oak.**

After six years of divorce and an extremely limited visitation schedule with my three treasured daughters, I had the chance to summon all of the Nehemiah-like powers I could scrape from the bottom of my spiritual reservoirs. This part of my life is called *I Won't Back Down*.

I WON'T BACK DOWN

I'm actually not a fighter. After a game of paintball with my older brother a few years back, I told him, "Listen, if we ever go to war I will be of no help to anyone if I get placed in the frontlines. I'm going to have to be working in the tents consoling those who have been wounded or something like that." I'm a highly sensitive person. I feel what others are feeling. I cry in movies. I reprimand kids when I see them messing with bugs. My heart can't stand to see anything or anyone in pain.

Being a pacifist has its downsides. It certainly did when I erringly thought that the more peaceful, kind and flexible I was toward my ex-wife at the beginning of our divorce, the more willing she'd be to work with me later down the road. I was dead wrong.

I started out agreeing to no overnights with my girls who were just five years old, three years old and an infant. After each daily phone call or video chat, I wept in extreme grief for the time I was missing out on and the memories that weren't being made. Then came the whiplash from spending every day of my life with these perfect littles and then never even being able to read them bedtime stories or kiss them goodnight.

After a year of this, I simply couldn't take it anymore. In my heart, I began to accept the truth that "backing down" all the time really didn't serve me or my children. I petitioned through the courts and was granted one overnight. I was grateful for the additional time, hoping for more in the future. With my new love, Chari, along with her two children that I now claimed, joyfully, as my own, we welcomed my daughters every other weekend for a twenty-seven-hour visit. We squeezed everything we possibly could out of this short time together, seeking to create a new "blended" (I actually hate that word) family culture.

And yet, one overnight is simply not enough to really feel like you're home or part of a family. That's what you do with friends at a sleepover or hanging out with Grandma and Grandpa. As positive as we tried to be in developing family traditions and lasting relationships, we struggled to get the traction we knew we needed.

We asked for more time, tried one additional overnight, and got lots of pushback. We were told that there was too much past trauma, that our home was not safe, that we were having a negative psychological impact on them. I knew it wasn't true. Although, I struggled to reject feelings of deep shame as I blamed myself for where we all had landed. We kept up the limited schedule for a couple more years until God shook me to a wakened state.

My eyes were opened to all of the hate going on in the world around me at that time. I watched in disbelief as the freedoms and liberties that are so often taken for granted in America slowly crumbled to pieces. It seemed like every political, social, race, health, environmental and religious issue was being polarized to a degree beyond peaceful resolve and coexistence. I felt like what was happening with my girls and their mom was just a microcosm of what was transpiring across the globe.

For the first time in my life, I felt gut-wrenching responsibility to take a stand and actually fight in a way that no one would be able to ignore. The words from Tom Petty's 1989 hit single, "I Won't Back Down," rocked my core as I drove home from my office on a hot summer day.

A new recognition was unfolding for me—that liberty is only preserved when coupled with responsibility. Conviction was setting in. And as I read from ancient scripture, I was reminded of the great Native American captain of war, Moroni. His words, piled on top of Tom Petty's, turned me into a modern-day Nehemiah:

Do ye supposed that the Lord will still deliver us, while we sit upon our thrones and do not make use of the means which the Lord has provided for us? Yea, will ye sit in idleness while ye are surrounded with thousands of those, yea, and tens of thousands, who do also sit in idleness…Do ye suppose that God will look upon you as guiltless while ye sit still and behold these things?… begin to be up and doing.[23]

Is there a word that's stronger than conviction? If there is, that's exactly where I was. As I counseled with my ever-steady support, Chari, I knew that if I truly wanted to fight for freedoms and God-given rights, I'd have to begin in my own home. We needed those girls to *actually* be a part of our family, not just visitors a couple times each month. This wall around our home, our family, our sanctuary had to be rebuilt and no one was going to do it for me.

I met with a new attorney to begin the case. When he looked at me and said, "Listen, I like you and you're a great guy, *and* I will fight to the gates of hell for your kids," I knew I had the right man for the job. We are still building this wall and while there are no guarantees, things are getting better and better. The flame of my faith burns bright as the words from my journal still illuminate my journey today:

> I'm no longer going to sit back as a pacifist, hoping and waiting for things to get better. I'm taking a stand for my little ones (Kella, Avery, and Taylen) by petitioning for more time. I'm taking a stand by teaching them how to fight for what matters to you. I'm not sure how this will play out regarding our country, liberties and freedoms, although I know this—it's time to make my voice be heard.
> I never want my kids to ask me, "Why didn't you fight for us? For our relationships, for our time, for our freedoms."

---

[23] Alma 60:21-24, The Book of Mormon.

No, I *won't* back down. No way, no how. I'm all in. I am doing a great work and I cannot come down.

This dynamic poem, by American writer Berton Braley, has a Nehemiah and Moroni-like ring to it. It has been a favorite of mine since I was nineteen. Here some of my favorite highlights from it:

"The Will to Win"

*If you want a thing bad enough
To go out and fight for it,
Work day and night for it,
…With all your capacity,
Strength and sagacity,
…Faith, hope and confidence,
If dogged and grim you besiege and beset it,
You'll get it!*

Nehemiah wanted it bad enough and got it. And so can you. Do you believe me? I'll tell you what, you might not believe me, and that's okay, because I believe me. You can ride on my coattails of belief for a bit. You've got it in you. There's a Life Mission that's been planted deep in your soul and when you've got it, you're golden. When we layer your values and principles on that Mission, then there is magic waiting to happen.

Journal Entry 🖊 *How bad do I want it? Am I willing to be all in like Nehemiah and say, "I'm doing a great work and cannot come down?" What would that kind of commitment take? Who could help me? What would happen if I showed up this way?*

So, one last time, are you willing to commit to your mission, principles and values? Yes? Excellent! Now, let's behold the magic as it beautifully unfolds.

CHAPTER SEVEN

Watching The Universe Align

*"You can't depend on your eyes when
your imagination is out of focus."*
—*Mark Twain*

Life Mission…check.

Principles and values…check.

Desire and dedication…check.

Now that you know what you want, all that's left is focus. Easier said than done, right? But it's true. Steve Jobs is accredited with the straightforward saying, "Focus is about saying 'no.'"[24] I like that. I like to think about it this way, "Focus is about saying 'yes.'" Let me explain with a fun story.

Brody Cole came into my life when he was a tiny, two-year-old toddler. He is, literally, my red-headed stepchild, but even now he possesses none of those stereotypical qualities. Brody is sweet, tender, loving, kind, respectful and an overall joy to have in my world.

One day, while attending a conference a few states away, I received a video of my then three-year-old daughter, Taylen, riding her bike with her stepdad. The training wheels had come off! Such a proud dad moment. As soon as I got home, I walked through the garage door and announced that four-year-old Brody would be losing the training wheels as well.

Before a welcoming hug or kiss, I got a glare and even a hand on the hip from my wife. "This is totally an ego thing," she inserted. "You're just pushing for this because Taylen did it and you don't want your son to be passed up by his little sister."

---

[24] https://www.youtube.com/watch?v=H8eP99neOVs
This is the video of Apple's 1997 Worldwide Developers Conference.

There may have been a small seed of truth to what she was saying. In any case, we were doing this! After a few minutes with the wrenches, the bike and boy were ready to go. Brody was eager with a smile of anticipation that lit up that cute little face. I was excited for this right-of-passage leading him from being a toddler right into boyhood. I handed him the red and white helmet, strapped it on and led him by the hand back inside to make final preparations.

I knelt down on one knee and looked him in the eyes. My hands rested on his shoulders as I outlined the simple and masterful plan I'd been conjuring up on the airplane.

"Okay, Bubbs," I began, using our favorite nickname for him, "riding your bike without training wheels is super easy. There are only three rules. . .okay?"

"Okay!" he agreed, with all the innocent faith of a little boy. So tender and sweet!

I shot one click glance up at Mom. "All right, Rule Number One: Mom gets to stay home while we go to the park. Sound good?"

"Yep!" All business from Brody. He was on board.

Mom rolled her eyes in the background, half smiling, which always meant she adored me and couldn't stand me all at the same time. Regardless, we were heading to the park.

We rolled up, put the SUV in park, got the bike out and walked over to the path. With the playground on one side and the grassy field on the other, our track was set.

Holding onto his handlebars and looking him square in the eyes, I continued to lay out our strategy. "Alright, Brody, you see that tree down there? Here's Rule Number Two: look at that tree. What's Rule Number Two?"

"Look at the tree!" The excitement was just about ready to boil over.

"You got it! Now, Rule Number Three: keep pedaling. What's Rule Number Three?"

"Keep pedaling!" He nailed it. He'd been waiting for this all his life.

"You see? It's easy. Number One. . .Mom's home and we're at the park. Number Two. . .Look at the tree. And Number Three. . .keep pedaling. You ready?"

"I'm ready!" And he certainly was.

Holding on to the back of his seat and running in the most awkward, bent-over, lunge position known to man, we were off.

"Look at the tree. Keep pedaling. Look at the tree. Keep pedaling," was my repeated mantra.

I let go with a prayer of hope and watched with wide eyes as he headed right for that tree. And that was the precise moment when I realized just how good of a coach I was. The success principle, "What you focus on expands" came screaming into my consciousness. I raced ahead as fast as my feet could fly and prevented what Mom had feared most.

Moral of the story: Moms are smarter than dads.

Secondary moral of the story: We get what we focus on consistently *or* what we focus on expands.

THE DYNAMIC POWER OF FOCUS

You see, Brody as a four-year-old, like all children between the ages of zero and eight, are in what's called *delta and theta brain-wave patterns*.[25] Kids are walking around like sponges, absorbing anything and everything. They are literally in the same brain-wave state as people under hypnosis. It's also the same brain-wave state as dream sleep.

Why does this matter? Well, if I had used "Focus is about saying 'no'" as a coaching strategy to help Brody, I would have gotten the exact opposite of what we'd come to do.

Let me explain. If I had said, "Whatever you do, don't turn around and look at me," what would he have done? Exactly! Turned around and looked at me. He would have wanted to know why not. What's back there? What am I missing out on? What happens if I turn around? And then his handlebars would have followed his head and he would have crashed.

---

[25] Lipton, B. (2005). The biology of belief: Unleashing the power of consciousness, matter and miracles. Santa Rosa, CA: Mountain of Love/Elite Books, p. 163.

What if I had said, "Don't stop pedaling?" He would have stopped. Is this because children are innately disobedient? No! The unconscious mind, which is what's in control when we're in high theta brain-wave patterns, will not process the negation in the sentence. It doesn't hear the "don't" and only hears what *not* to do.

This is why when you yell at a kid, "Don't touch that!" they always touch it. Or how about, "Don't drop that!" What happens?

Let's try an experiment...

Don't think about a pink elephant with purple polka dots. How did you do? You see, you're not much better off than a four-year-old!

If we focus on moving away from what we don't want, we give energy and attention to what we don't want. And then we wonder why. *What's wrong with me? Why do I keep getting what I don't want in my life?* Simple, your unconscious mind does not process the negation and so you're actually commanding it to do the opposite of what you want.

As a life coach, I have learned that a far greater majority of people are moving away from what they don't want in life compared to those who are moving toward what they do want. Here's what this sounds like:

"I just don't want to be so dang tired all the time."

"I don't want to be broke."

"I wish I didn't have to work overtime."

"I'd love to not have to always be the one to apologize first in my relationship."

"I don't want to look in the mirror and hate my body."

"I never want to talk about or get a divorce."

Think about those you know who are most miserable and unhappy in their life. Do they focus on what they want? Do they talk about their goals, ambitions, hopes and dreams or are they mostly complaining, telling you everything they *don't* want in their life?

Remember Brody's two rules and mantra: Look at the tree. Keep pedaling.

A strong tree also has two rules it follows:

Number One--Roots. Soak up water and nutrients from the soil to provide a steady support.

Number Two--Leaves. Produce food for the tree through photosynthesis by absorbing light.

That's all it wants. Can you imagine a tree saying the following?

This dirt is so cold and dark and every time it rains I'm surrounded by mud. I wish I didn't have to be down here. I hope I don't drown. I don't want to be the smallest, weakest tree in the forest. I wish I wasn't growing so slowly. I don't want to be under another big tree. They'll take up all the light.

Nature is a beautiful example of moving toward what it wants.

I'm soaking up everything I can get from this mud. I'm so grateful to be down here. I hope it rains all day! I'm going to grow as big as I possibly can. It's going to take some time and I'm alright with that. I trust the process. I sure am glad to be under that big tree. It gives me something to look up to. I'm going to take in all I can as I learn from one of the greats.

You can say 'yes' every day to your roots, your Life Mission. Focus on the values and principles you know will guarantee your success. Write them down. Frame them. Write poems. Put them on your bathroom mirror. Use sticky notes to decorate your house, car, office. Break out some sidewalk chalk and declare your intentions to the whole neighborhood! Whatever it takes, focus on what you want. When you do, everything else will fall out of your world or right into its proper place. Watch the Universe align for you to fulfill what you were created to be, do and have here on this planet.

> *"Where focus goes, energy flows. And where energy flows, whatever you're focusing on grows.... your life is controlled by what you focus on."*
> —Tony Robbins

Journal Entry 🖉 *How's my focus? What can I do to better move toward what I want? How will this slight shift in attention impact my greatest goals and desires? How could I create daily routines and practices that best help me keep this focus?*

FORGET THE FOCUS

"The greatness of a man's power is the
measure of his surrender."
—William Booth

Do you remember being a little kid and working so hard to get to the point where you could finally take that one last hand off of your handlebars and ride hands free? "Look, Mom! No hands!" As liberating and exhilarating as that feels for a child, it's as equally terrifying to watch as a parent. I don't have a cute dad coaching story about me teaching my kids how to do this. It scares the heck out of me!

There's an innocent and authentic faith in that moment though. The child trusts her capabilities, lets go of the fear, relinquishes control, and allows the momentum of the moment, literally, to carry her forward. Wind in the face. Letting go feels so good.

A **Strength of the Oak** commitment to and focus on what matters most is absolutely essential. And so is surrendering. **Strength of the Willow**.

Surrendering, as William Booth reminded us, is an indication of great power. Unfortunately, we all too often assume that it's an act of weakness, a floundering, lifeless, abandonment of courage, a white flag of failure. How sad.

When we break down the origin of the word *surrender*, we find the French *sur,* meaning "over" and *rendre,* meaning "to give back."[26] To

---

[26] https://www.etymonline.com/word/surrender

surrender is to give something back *over*, rather than giving *up*. When we surrender, we can turn our plans, our goals, our vision, our mission over to something and someone far greater than us. We forget ourselves and let go of the "arm of flesh," our own mortal strengths and we rely upon the giver of the gifts.

Now, unless YOU created YOU, then something or someone else deserves the credit. I heard this idea presented for the first time by Gary Keller, who is the founder of Keller Williams Realty International, the largest real estate company in the world. He taught that unless we created ourselves, we must submit to something greater, whether that's God or the Universe.

Either of those choices is pretty powerful and it's even more powerful when we remember that surrendering is not giving up, it's not defeat, it's giving ourselves over to a higher power. I love that word, *over*. To me, it implies that God is right next to me in my life, just *over* there. He's my teammate. We're in this to win.

In baseball, when the starting pitcher is struggling on the mound, the coach brings in a fresh arm from the bull-pen. The worn-out pitcher hands the ball *over* to the relief pitcher. I love this exchange. I imagine one of two things going on in the mind of the starting pitcher:

Mindset #1:

"Man! I let the team down. Why doesn't Coach trust me to finish the job? Now I gotta give this ball up because I couldn't get it done."

This is selfish thinking. The pitcher is assuming that he had to carry the team by himself. The error in this reasoning is the false expectation of having to complete the entire game as the sole pitcher. In actuality, this only happens about 1% of the time. The other 99% of games are pitched by two or more players.

Mindset #2:

"Alright...I gave it my all. I know I did my best. So grateful to give this ball over to my teammate who I can count on. He's going to help our team close out this game on top."

Selfless thinking. This starting pitcher understands his limits and doesn't expect more than what he was able to give. He relies on others to win. Simon Sinek says, "A team is not a group of people that work together. A team is a group of people that trust each other."[27] The starting pitcher must trust the relief pitcher.

So, where does your trust lie? Are you still trying to grit and grind your way through life on your own, focused solely on you, your capabilities and what you want? Are you attempting, all by yourself, to pitch a perfect game, even though there's already been a few runs scored against you and the scoreboard's not looking so good?

The **Strength of the Oak** holds on for dear life, never letting go no matter what. That's the kind of strength that gets the proverbial monkey stuck with its hand in the trap, unwilling to drop the nut so that he can pull his hand out of the hole. Let go!

It's the water skier being pulled behind the ski boat, having fallen, most likely having lost their skis (and maybe their shorts too), swallowing gallons of water as they're being dragged head first through the lake. Let go!

The **Strength of the Willow**, on the other hand, understands that we waste a lot of energy trying in vain to hold on to fistfuls of goopy slime. The harder you squeeze, the more you lose. **The Strength of the Willow** trusts that by letting go, there's freedom on the other side. It's an exercise of strength conservation. It's surrendering to what empowers us to get back up and try again.

At the end of each calendar year, I challenge my clients (and my own children) to create a vision board for what an amazingly

---

[27] https://twitter.com/simonsinek/status/232556392114974721?lang=en
1:18 PM · Aug 6, 2012.

productive, rewarding and fulfilling life will look like for the upcoming year. It's a simple and fun way to get clarity on who we desire to be, what we intend to do and what we'd like to have in our lives. I also created one myself. In December of 2018, I texted Chari, asking her to send me a picture of a house that I could print off and stick on my vision board. We were looking forward to selling our first home together and moving into something more spacious for our five kids and sixth that was on his way.

She sent over a house, I printed it out, pasted it on the vision board, and forgot about it until I got home later that day. In that sacred hour or two when kids are in bed and we get to sit down and connect, I asked, "Hey, tell me about that house I put on my vision board today." She pulled up the exact property online that was for sale and I gasped when I saw the price tag. "Are you kidding me? We can't afford that." She looked at me with those big brown eyes and said, sweetly, "You always seem to find a way to make things happen." I really don't like it when she says that.

Not only was the home a bit pricier than I'd been wanting to pay, it had been on the market for two months already and we weren't looking to move for another three. I told her there was very little chance that it would even be around when it was time to start shopping. "Don't get your hopes up, Honey."

That home sat on my vision board for the next month, out of sight and out of mind. It also sat on the market. After closing out all of my 2018 books and chatting with my lender, she informed me that we actually *did* qualify to purchase in that price range. We got a babysitter for a date night, went out to dinner and scheduled a showing with our real estate agent—me! As we passed from room to room, I knew pretty quickly that Chari had made up her mind. This home was going to be ours.

It was time to make things happen.

I pulled out all the stops, reached into my bag of negotiation tricks, turned it all over to God, and said to my sweet wife, "If it's to be, it's no longer up to me." I surrendered. We knew what we wanted, we did all we could and we left the outcome in the hands of a higher power.

In March of 2019, we walked through that home once again, this time as the owners, not the wishful buyers. I literally cried in a state of gratitude and overwhelm for this dream house and the life we'd be building within. Two weeks later, I was in tears one more time as I held our newborn boy, Jacob, and welcomed him into our home. Oh, and by the way, we put a little boy on that vision board as well.

I've heard it said that two people can accomplish anything, as long as one of those people is God. Let go, let God. That child-like faith can carry you a long way. Jesus, take the handlebars!

Journal Entry 🖊 *What is it costing me to not let go?*

There's someone reading this right now who's got this unanswered question nagging at them. "But, how? I get this whole surrendering, turning things over to God and the Universe thing, conceptually. But how? How do I actually do it? How do I let go of what I want?"

CREATING SPACE

Mother Earth often teaches some of the most profound sermons in so very few words. When I stop and appreciate the beauties of all that this world has to offer, I'm astounded. The power of the lessons taught blow any classroom out of the water.

The late Hugh B. Brown, attorney, educator, author and spiritual leader told the following story of a carelessly kept farm he purchased in Canada. The impact this has had on my life has been so great that I share my summary below:

He stepped outside one morning to find a currant bush that had grown to over six feet tall. With no signs of blossom or fruit, it seemed to be nothing but a giant weed. Having grown up on a fruit farm of his father's, he'd had adequate experience when it came to pruning trees. He pulled out his pruning shears and started clipping until it was cut down to just about nothing but a small bunch of stumps.

As he looked at what was left, he gave in to a common and silly impulse he often had, to talk to inanimate objects and let them talk back. Before saying anything, he seemed to catch sight of a tear or two on each stump. He asked that little currant bush what was wrong and what it was crying about.

The response came in a somber inquiry as to why and how he could be doing such a thing to a helpless victim like itself. It was as if it were saying, "My growth was wonderful. I had almost reached the same stature as the other trees in the garden and here you come cutting me down. All will now look down upon me with pity. How in the world could you do this to me? You're supposed to be my caretaker."

He then answered:

> *Look, little currant bush, I am the gardener here, and*
> *I know what I want you to be. If I let you go the way*
> *you want to go, you will never amount to anything. But*
> *someday, when you are laden with fruit, you are going*
> *to think back and say, "Thank you, Mr. Gardener, for*
> *cutting me down, for loving me enough to hurt me."*[28]

Honestly, aren't we all like that little currant bush, to some extent? We grow and grow and grow some more, thinking we're becoming and doing all that we are capable of. And then, something happens, we get cut down, our life doesn't go as planned and we curse God, the great Gardener of the Universe as if to say, "I know better!"

Why does it have to be this way? Why the pruning? More than anything, that little currant bush needed space and light to one day be laden with fruit. Like that little bush, letting go of what we want means listening more than talking, trusting more than willing, accepting more than demanding, learning more than leading. What would a solitary word be that could aptly describe the depth of strength that's possible here? You tell me:

---

[28] https://speeches.byu.edu/talks/hugh-b-brown/god-gardener/

Meekness. Yielding. Faith. Hope. Surrender. Flow. Harmony. Peace. Stillness. Flexible. Gentle. Acceptance. Temperate. Gradual. Patient. Ease. Serenity.

Those who seem to grow into the greatest measure of their creation carry this hidden humility, almost imperceptible, and definitely undeclared. It's a humility which recognizes that by ourselves, we are nothing. **Strength of the Willow.** And in order to come to this place, we need space. Pruning is of the essence.

CHAPTER EIGHT

The Power of Joy and Gratitude

"So often we think that joy makes us grateful,
when in reality it's gratitude that brings joy."
—Brené Brown

I remember one day sitting down, on vacation, and watching TV (a rare occasion) while our baby boy, Jacob, napped. This was the first time I had been introduced to Marie Kondo, the tidying expert, bestselling author, and as I was about to learn, star of Netflix's hit show, "Tidying Up With Marie Kondo."

Curiosity overcame me as she walked into a household with a husband and wife who were on the verge of becoming the next home on "Hoarders." In her brilliantly soft-spoken way, Marie explained, "The best way to choose what to keep and what to throw away is to take each item in one's hand and ask, 'Does this spark joy?' If it does, keep it. If not, dispose of it. This is not only the simplest but also the most accurate yardstick by which to judge."

Whoa! "Does this spark joy?" So simple and so applicable to all things in life, not just material items in our home.

Letting go and creating space for something magnificent, beyond even our greatest imagination, is as easy as asking, "Does this spark joy in my life?" And if the answer is not a resounding "Yes!" then we know it is taking up needed space and energy, suffocating future possibilities.

But how do you know if something or someone holds a place of joy in your life? Does it *have* to be a spark? Could it be something less dramatic? Certainly. We could just as easily call it a blanket of joy, rather than a spark. I actually really like the idea of a spark because you *know* when there's a spark happening--you see it, sometimes even hear it and you might even feel it.

I also really like the idea of a blanket of joy. Sometimes, in the middle of the night, you don't consciously feel the blanket until it's gone and a slight shiver rattles you awake. I believe that's how joy can be too. Sometimes we're not aware of a subtle joy in our life until it's been removed, but oh, can we feel the cold!

The warmth of joy could also be compared to that feeling you have when you hold an infant and you just can't help but smile. A lot of people feel a similar emotion while holding a puppy or a kitten. It's a very grounding place to be. It's as if time stops, worries cease and all that matters in the world is right there in your arms.

You also know it's joy when that feeling lingers. There's not a crash afterward like you'd experience in a hangover or after eating too much sugary dessert. Joy holds a place in our heart that only invites, never demands more. That invitation calls for us to make a choice, a choice to be happy.

I learned this from "The Velvet Hammer," a woman who received this nickname because of the incredible love, care and candor she brought as a leader. Her name was Mo Anderson and she served as the CEO of Keller Williams Realty for over ten years.

My first introduction to Mo was in a video during a training I was taking. I've since seen that video several times and her strong Oklahoma accent has been imprinted on my mind for years to come. "When I act enthusiastic, I will be enthusiastic!" which she emphatically repeated over and over. Given all that was happening in my world at that time, I was *not* always enthusiastic about living in my parents' basement, being divorced, "grounded" and feeling like my life was hanging by a thread.

Now however, whenever I was feeling down and my energy was low, Mo's voice would go through my head, *"When I act enthusiastic, I will be enthusiastic!"*

People would ask, "How are you doing today, Andrew?" and I started answering, "I'm happy!" They'd cock their head to the side, a bit bewildered as this was new for me, and it wasn't a common response you get from anyone. Some would even laugh and reply, "I like that answer," or "I've never heard anyone say that before." It's a simple response that I still employ today. And the amazing thing about it is that when you say you're happy, you actually start to feel happy!

I've never been a huge fan of the phrase, "Fake it till you make it." That's not what this is about. It's more of an, "Act as if." I could go endlessly into studies that show what this acting as if does to a human's biochemistry, but I won't. I will tell you this: if we authentically act in a manner of joy and happiness, telling ourselves and others that this is the state we *choose* to live in, then we find ourselves taking actions accordingly.

For one thing, I can't say those words without smiling. I rapidly discovered that what the Velvet Hammer spoke was true: those actions strengthen neural pathways of belief, therefore creating more, good-feeling chemicals. Happiness can be a choice. It was for me and it transformed everything...

So, I invite you to take a serious look at your life right now and ask, "What am I pretending to ignore that is not sparking joy in my life today?" You just thought of at least one thing. . .I know you did. What else? Now, this is one of the moments where you can decide to keep reading and not do the work because you just want to get through the book. And I again plead with you to *pause*. . .Take some time here to journal, make a list, sit back and ponder or ask a loved one that same question, in order for you to gain insight into what you might not be seeing.

Journal Entry ✎ *Now, this is the time for you to go deep. "What in my life am I pretending to ignore that is not bringing joy to me today?"*

I'm not saying this is going to be easy. You may recognize that this something or someone has a high level of attachment for you. It might be as big as your job, career or business. It could be as important as a relationship with a significant other, spouse, child, sibling or parent. It may also be a tightly woven habit like smoking, drinking, pornography, drugs, gambling, eating or some other slippery vice.

And I'll tell you what, your ego is going to fight with everything it's got to defend whatever or whoever this is. And when I talk about ego here,

I'm not referring to the cocky, letterman jacket wearing, high school kid or the mean girl who thinks she's better than everyone else. In the field of psychology, your ego is who you think you are and really aren't. It's a false identity and it has one single, solitary and selfish goal: STAY ALIVE! And when you identify something that is not bringing you joy and it is, in all actuality, *killing* your higher self, your ego is going to throw the biggest fit you've ever seen. You're going to hear every excuse, justification and reason as to why you need to hang on to this false hope. Your ego's negotiating skills will make any toddler or teenage tantrum you've witnessed seem like a peaceful Sunday morning.

This is going to be a defining moment, a turning point in your life. You get to take full inventory and ownership of your happiness and make a conscious decision as to whether or not you will allow anything other than joy to fill your inner space.

As my dear friend and brilliant artist, Giotta Vorgia, once said, "Never let anyone else choose what goes into your space."

Let me be perfectly clear. You were born to live in joy. It is indeed your birthright. Just as a tender sapling is dependent on sunlight to survive and thrive, you are dependent upon joy. When the shades of uncertainty and doubt and comparison and rationalization are preventing you from soaking in the rays of light and joy, you must remove that obstruction!

So, I'm going to ask you, one more time, with all the coaching passion I can muster over here in my corner, yelling out to your great and powerful spirit: WHAT CAN YOU SEE IN YOUR LIFE RIGHT NOW THAT IS NOT BRINGING YOU JOY?

It's time for you to take a stand for *you*. Pull out those pruning shears and create some space. It's time to let joy in.

Journal Entry 🖋 *You now know what's not bringing you joy and messing with the sacred space in your life. What's your plan to remove it? What will this entail? Who will best be able to support you in doing so? What's the first step? When, exactly, are you going to take it? What will this do for your soul? What will you see when this space is clear? What will that feel like? Who will thank you most for making this tough and loving decision? What will this have done for your character when completed? What will you be able to say, one day, years down the road, as you look back at this turning point in your life?*

GRATITUDE: NATURE'S SUNLIGHT

Let's explore the miracle of the sun for just a moment. Earth travels in an elliptical, not completely circular, path around the sun. This means that the distance between Earth and the sun changes throughout the year. Did you know the sun is 91.4 million miles away from us, at its closest point, and 94.5 million miles away at its farthest? In eight minutes, traveling at 186,000 miles per second, light arrives from the sun to our home we call Earth.[29]

Upon arrival, this light energy, carried across the immensity of space, touches all living things. For plants, this sunlight is absorbed by chlorophyll and begins the process we know as photosynthesis. Next, water, absorbed from the ground, along with carbon dioxide, taken in from the air, are changed into oxygen, which is released for our livelihood.

We, like plants, also have the divinely creative ability to take in everything around us and use it for an inside out kind of self-transformation. We can be as resourceful as plants, if we adopt the following mindset:

LIFE EVENTS ARE NOT HAPPENING *TO* US;
THEY ARE HAPPENING *FOR* US!

I witnessed this in a rather sobering conversation with a client I've grown to respect and adore. Let's call her Ashley.

Ashley stepped in, big time, as her mom, dad and sister had been working tirelessly through the challenges of their adult brother and son's

---

[29] https://coolcosmos.ipac.caltech.edu/ask/8-How-far-away-is-the-Sun-

journey with ALS. It had been over a year and half since the diagnosis. Travis was now bedridden and 100% dependent upon others for his care. Watching her parents' physical, mental and emotional exhaustion, Ashley and her sister began taking shifts to relieve Mom and Dad. She eventually helped pay for a nurse to further aid in the daily duties of ensuring her brother was as comfortable and as well-taken care of as possible.

I asked her, "Ashley, you guys have been through so much. Why do you believe this is happening *for* you and your family right now?"

She replied, "Well, the other day I received a text from Travis. He can no longer communicate verbally. He has lost all motor skills and now uses an on-screen keyboard that allows him to type by selecting letters with his eyes. His message said, 'It's literally harder to stay alive now. Everything is tougher to do. Everything.'

"In response I actually thanked him for this whole experience and shared my love for him. I told him that he's the strongest person I know. I told him how much I'd learned and how blessed we as a family had been since all of this happened. As I explained to him, Andrew, we've seen miracles as extended family feuds have been set aside and long-lost relationships have been restored. Our faith in God has increased exponentially. We are closer and have sacrificed in a way that has strengthened our love like never before.

"He replied to her tender words with, 'Thank you Ashley. I'm literally trying not to cry. I love you too!'"

Her story tugged at my heartstrings and I listened in awe as I watched her hardships being transformed into gratitude. Healing was happening for her and her family in unexpected and previously unthinkable ways. And her brother was able to witness what could have easily been seen as an unbearable burden become a beacon of hope for all around him. This illness had miraculously turned from "a destructive disease happening to us" to "a sanctifying experience happening for us."

I honor and admire Ashley, her family, along with any and all who endure challenges of this nature. It is beyond humbling to observe the breakdowns and breakthroughs that accompany these life-altering experiences.

Melody Beattie, best-selling self-help author, taught:

*"Gratitude unlocks the fullness of life. It turns
what we have into enough, and more…
Gratitude makes sense of our past, brings peace for
today and creates a vision for tomorrow. Gratitude makes
things right. Gratitude turns negative energy into positive
energy. There is no situation or circumstance so small or
large that it is not susceptible to gratitude's power."*[30]

THE SCIENCE OF GRATITUDE

These kinds of gratitude stories, like Ashley's, don't just feel good for storytelling's sake. There's some science behind what's going on here.

You see, gratitude has the capacity to increase important neuro-chemicals. As we mentally shift from the negative to the positive, a surge of feel-good hormones takes place. Dopamine, serotonin and oxytocin all contribute to the feelings of connection and camaraderie, willpower and motivation, optimism and joy.[31]

As humans, we have the creative powers to transform potentially destructive "negative" experiences into life-changing and defining moments. Plants can do it, and *must* do it to survive. You can too. And you must; there's too much at stake if you don't.

It's a decision, that's all there is to it. Will I allow my reptilian brain to drag me down a path toward a pity party where "Woe Is Me" is the only guest to RSVP? Or will I slow down, flip the switch and ask, "Why is this happening *for* me right now in my life?" You'll be shocked at what you'll find and how you'll thrive by making this one small change.

This simple switch brought a good friend of mine up pretty fast after a long-term girlfriend unexpectedly ended their relationship. His answer to my question, "Why is this happening *for* you right now?" ran through

---

[30] https://melodybeattie.com/gratitude-2/
[31] https://positivepsychology.com/neuroscience-of-gratitude/

his head for days and weeks afterward, "So I don't have to spend another day or year with someone who doesn't want to be with me."

"Aren't you grateful to know that?" I replied.

His hug said it all. Spark of joy. Blanket of comfort. **Strength of the Willow**.

Journal Entry 🖊 *Can you remember a time in your life that may have seemed very confusing and downtrodden when you were going through it? Are you able to see, with a different perspective now, how that event helped mold and develop you into the person you are today? Why do you believe that happened for you at that specific time in your life? Are you experiencing something right now that could benefit from a shift in perspective now rather than later? I invite you to write about it and see what lessons you can pull away as to why this is happening for you in your life right now.*

APPLIED GRATITUDE: SCUBA STYLE

So, what are you grateful for? I invite you, right here, to jot down at least five things you're grateful for.

5 Things I'm Grateful For

1) _____

2) _____

3) _____

4) _____

5) _____

Look back over that list and think about each one for just a moment. Congratulations! This is what I call "surface gratitude." You've skimmed across the top of the water. It's a nice place to be. Now, let's go just a little bit deeper.

I call this next part "snorkeling." Let's stick your head under the surface of gratitude and see what's down there. Why are you grateful for each of those specifically? Write them down. If you said, "My family," your why might be something like, "because they showed up last week when I needed them most."

Or maybe you wrote down, "My shoes," and your why could be, "because I look and feel amazing when I'm wearing them!" Expressing why you're grateful takes us further from a cognitive level to an even more profound, emotional level of thanks. It connects the dots between what you're grateful for and how it's actually shaping your life.

Why I'm Grateful for Each

1) _____

_____

2) _____

_____

3) _____

_____

4) _____

_____

5) _____

_____

Now, we're going to scuba dive. Take a good, deep breath and get ready for some magic. If there's a person on that list, we're going to give them this gift of gratitude. If there's not a person and only things, animals, etc., think about who gave each to you or see if you can somehow connect it to someone. Maybe there's a memory with someone that's associated with whatever you wrote down.

Pull out your phone and make a call, send a text, write an email or a thank-you note or make a visit to their home or office. Choose one person that you commit to sharing this appreciation with, today. (Now's a good time, too...wink, wink...)

Allowing others to understand the role they've played in our quest for a joyful life enhances their own personal gratification. They probably felt an initial, sincere joy in giving you that gift or in sharing that memory. Coming back around to remind them of how their generosity continues to bless your life today is like pulling back the inevitable weeds to reveal the flower planted last year.

You have now multiplied the power of giving and the immediate joy that follows!

Now that you've dived down and shared this appreciation, it's time to go back up and really seal the deal. This last step is the capstone of gratitude.

Let's think about plants and sunlight one more time. Wouldn't it be cool to find out that somehow plants and the sun actually were able to communicate with each other. Maybe a plant would say, each and every morning as the sun wakes up the world, "Thank you, Mr. Sun, for helping to make me what I am today!" And maybe the sun would reply, "My pleasure!"

And if that plant were connected in an even higher spiritual manner, maybe it would then honor the Creator of the sun and offer a simple prayer with words like, "Thank you, God, for making the sun what it is today."

As we honor the One who gave us that person, we are at one with the powers of creation and rest in a state of flow, not force. And flow is abundant. Like the waves of the ocean, there is never a shortage of what it can give or the possibility for more.

Go ahead and take a moment to pause, whether it's a short and sweet prayer of thanks or a moment of meditation, and give that gift of gratitude up to a higher source or wherever you feel most connected.

This final step really seals the deal and creates an anchored state of appreciation beyond the surface level recognition in our own mind as to the good around us. It is one thing to acknowledge our gratitude, and quite another to write it down, explore why we feel the way we do, share this with someone who played a part in it and then connect that gratitude with a higher source.

As you build a daily habit of following these 4 Steps of Applied Gratitude, I promise that you will experience a level of joy you never knew possible.

4 Steps of Applied Gratitude

1. **Write down at least five gratitudes.**
2. **Why are you grateful for each?**
3. **Share this gratitude with at least one person.**
4. **Honor the One who gave you this person.**

My invitation to you is to make a game out of this. Don't like playing games? Okay, let's call it an experiment. Too nerdy? Fine, it's a challenge!

Take three to five minutes each day and go through the Four Steps of Applied Gratitude. Do it for a week and then a month, and if you really want to see some intense transformation and joy, keep going! You decide.

If you go two months and don't see a drastic shift in the degree to which you experience joy, then you reach out to me and I'll personally help you release whatever's getting in your way. My email's in the back of the book. I'm here for you. I believe in this stuff. It has changed millions of lives for the better and that means it will change yours too.

In those dark days of living in my parents' basement, my daily gratitudes helped ground me in a way that I didn't fully comprehend at the time. As I look back on my journaled gratitudes, I can clearly see how that simple practice kept the spark and hope of joy alive for me when almost everything else seemed to be doing the exact opposite.

"I would maintain that thanks are the highest form of thought; and that gratitude is happiness doubled by wonder."
—G.K. Chesterton

CHAPTER NINE

The Power of Your Presence

"You are not a human doing. You are a human being."
—Every New Age, enlightened, spiritual teacher

plat·i·tude
/ˈpladə͟ˌt(y) o͞od/
noun
1. a remark or statement, especially one with a moral content, that has been used too often to be interesting or thoughtful.[32]

There are piles of books, blogs, articles and podcasts that will teach you the principles of *being* versus *doing*. Each author will lead you along an untethered path where your soul can tap into the power held in the now and you can start to think like a monk. In all seriousness, these resources are worth every penny and second you can pour into them. You will receive priceless wisdom on how to be aware and present through meditation and other in-depth practices.

My purpose here is not to regurgitate these, restating them in my own words. What I'm yearning for is a revelation, an unveiling of what's possible for YOU when you realize your powerful presence. To get there, we've got to machete our way through some thick stuff. So, let's go…

I want you to think about what happens when you're first introduced to a new acquaintance. You'll often hear things like, "What do you do for a living?" or "What do you like to do in your spare time?" We have been conditioned to search for someone's identity in their behaviors, what they do. The problem? We seem to correlate personas, social facades and the public roles we play with our higher selves, as if we *are* those labels. Sure, these labels help us make quick associations

---

[32] https://www.google.com/search?q=platitude+definition&oq=paltitude&aqs=chrome.2.69i57j0i10i433i512l2j0i10i512l7.3063j0j7&sourceid=chrome&ie=UTF-8

and initial judgments. Can I connect with this person? Do we have anything in common? Do we belong here together?

Yet, take those labels away and who are you? Forget work and hobbies. Now who are you? Do you have a hard time answering that question? There are layers to our identity and our labels that have to be sifted through. Consider jotting down the labels you wear on a day-to-day basis. Gather all of the labels that you and others use to describe you.

- At Work– Are you the Boss? Employee? Senior Manager? Office clown? Paper pusher?
- At Home– Cat lady? Dog lover? Gardener? Pool boy? Janitor? Chef? Chauffeur?
- In Your Family– Brother/Sister? Spouse? Grandparent? Mom? Dad? Cousin? Aunt? Uncle?
- Recreation– Fantasy Football King? Water Boy? Surfer? Quilter? Yogi? Artist? Musician?

My Labels

_____	_____	_____
_____	_____	_____
_____	_____	_____
_____	_____	_____
_____	_____	_____

Take a look. Who are you without them? Seriously. How do you describe yourself *without those words?* If we struggle to answer this paramount question, then we've fallen victim to this social conditioning that states, "We are only as good as the hats we wear."

We can really start to lose ourselves in this kind of thinking. When we're drowning in these turbulent waters, it is saddening to see

THE POWER OF YOUR PRESENCE

someone so unknowingly misled. I can say that because I've been there too. And I clawed my way out of it. An all-time favorite quote will help. I actually love this so much that I've committed it to memory and share it with as many as will listen. It's from Marianne Williamson's masterpiece, *A Return to Love*:

> *"Our deepest fear is not that we are inadequate. Our deepest fear is that we are powerful beyond measure. It is our light, not our darkness that most frightens us. We ask ourselves, 'Who am I to be brilliant, gorgeous, talented, fabulous?' Actually, who are you not to be?"*

Let me ask you, who are you without those labels? How about powerful beyond measure? Brilliant, gorgeous, talented, fabulous? A child of God? Born to make manifest the glory of God that is within you? A liberating presence? Yes! Those words! Powerful! She goes on to say:

> *"We were born to make manifest the glory of God that is within us. It's not just in some of us; it's in everyone. And as we let our own light shine, we unconsciously give other people permission to do the same. As we are liberated from our own fear, our presence automatically liberates others."*[33]

Thank you, Marianne Williamson! Your very words breathe life into my soul.

And so, to you the reader, one more time, who are you without your labels? When that raw and exposed you is open to the world, do you feel powerful beyond measure? Can you look into the mirror and say, "You know what, I *am* brilliant, gorgeous, talented and fabulous?" Do you know, beyond the shadow of a doubt, that you are a child of Divine Parentage, born to make manifest the glory of godliness that is within you? Are you free from fear and therefore a liberating presence to others?

---

[33] 1992, A Return to Love: Reflections on the Principles of A Course in Miracles by Marianne Williamson, Chapter 7: Work, Quote Page 165, Published by HarperCollins, New York.

If you could boldly and humbly say 'yes' to all of those questions, what would that mean? Really, what would it mean to you to be able to wake up each day and affirm with unquestionable certainty:

→ **I am indeed powerful beyond measure!**
→ **I am brilliant, gorgeous, talented and fabulous!**
→ **I am a child of God (a great creator, divine love, a universal intelligence...you choose).**
→ **I was born to make manifest the glory of godliness that is within me.**
→ **I am free from fear and my presence automatically liberates others.**

If you read those affirmations out loud and they don't vibrate on your frequency and you feel like they just don't fit, then we've got some more ego to get rid of. Those *other* labels that you've been branded with throughout your life are not who you are. These are truth.

Let me tell you about the strength of the adhesive backing all of those other labels. Think about duct tape, superglue and epoxy all combined together and then take that and multiply it by *a thousand* and you'll be getting closer to the power of ego-held beliefs and labels. This is not like ripping off a band-aid. This is like pulling away what seems to be a very real part of you, so much so that it might literally feel as if you are, in all actuality, dying.

So, here's the good news: You're not dying! And it doesn't have to hurt. The old adage "No pain, no gain" does not have to be true for you. You can drop your ego faster than your junior high fling. It's a choice and I'd like to walk you through how simple it can be.

But before we do, I'd like to share the story as to how this book came to be. This is a small glimpse into how I've personally experienced a resounding, **Strength of the Oak** wake-up call as to who I am beneath all of my labels. The vulnerable experience I'm about to share was a defining moment for my life. It was when and where I unequivocally came to a realization of my powerful, liberating presence.

REVELATION IN ZION

It was Friday, February 28, 2020, just days before the world would soon be sucker punched in the face by a fear-laden, silently invisible enemy that was to become the 2020 Pandemic. I was attending a personal development, life mastery retreat in St. George, Utah that would turn out to be one of the most significant, transformative events of my life.

I went into the weekend with an open mind, knowing that if the hand of Providence had something to deliver, I would be more than happy to receive it. I was that open. I also, somewhat naively, wondered how my life could get any better.

The previous year I had accomplished what at one time had seemed utterly impossible. I'd worked fewer days and hours than I'd ever worked in any given year up to that point. I had made more money than I'd ever made before and helped more people than I'd ever helped. I stayed home and didn't travel for business once that year. I had set an intention that I would be there for my sixth child, Jacob's, entire first year of life. And I did it. I was present, and I celebrated that.

My 2019 vision had come to fruition. I was on cruise control. And yet, I had been pulled by thoughts as to the future direction of my career and how I could maximize my efforts and potential to live out my Life Mission.

The other retreat attendees and I took a chartered bus from St. George up into the world-famous Zion National Park. I had never quite understood why people loved this area so much. They had spoken of its sacredness, the healing powers there and the magnificent landscape. I'd always been a bit underwhelmed by this part of the country. I'm an Idaho boy who loves and appreciates the Rocky Mountains with their green pines, crystal clear lakes and the animal life that so easily befriends you in those welcoming forests. And then again, I'd never actually set foot in or spent time in these rather dry, desert canyons. I'd only driven through once or twice. So, maybe I was being a little too hard on this place. I *had* promised myself to be open.

We unloaded from the tour bus and I sat down, alone, on a cool cement bench to eat my sack lunch. One of the other attendees, Melissa, walked up, with a smile on her face, and asked if she could join me. I scooted over and she sparked up a conversation, posing a string of poignant, provoking questions.

"Andrew, have you written a book?"

I shook my head.

"No? Why not?" I couldn't answer that.

Then she asked, "Do you speak professionally? No? Why not?"

As I fumbled my way through what I believed to be decent reasons, Melissa pointed out that my reasons sounded a lot more like lame excuses to her. I was surprised by her boldness as usually *I* was the one making others feel uncomfortable in that kind of a coaching setting. And now here I was, with my hiney in the hot seat. My insides were writhing, my head was spinning and my knee was bouncing up and down a million miles an hour, anxiously hoping that there wouldn't be any more questions in this interrogation. *Why was I so uneasy?*

For as long as I can remember, I've had a clarity and confidence of my capabilities to show up, in just about any circumstance, as a leader. I know how to get stuff done and engage others to join me. Through my formative years of childhood, adolescence and young adulthood, I learned to mask this strength, to play smaller than the force inside that always seemed to yell, "Get up! Go first! Volunteer! Lead the way! You know what to do." I was afraid of others' perceptions. I didn't want to come across as too much, too powerful, a manipulator or just downright pushy. So, I got really good at holding back the innate leader's drive inside of me.

Melissa wasn't buying it and the thought of unmasking this suppressed superhero and putting him on the world's stage by speaking and writing was freaking me out.

Somehow, I pulled myself together and politely thanked her for opening up my mind. I was more than happy to be parting ways. Yet, her thoughts she left with me lingered restlessly for a few moments, until they slowly drifted away as I intentionally shifted my focus to take in the scenery that surrounded me. Distraction, my trickster of a cohort, could unquestionably be counted on to quiet that calling.

In my discomfort, I decided to take a short stroll up the canyon and down to the Virgin River. I cranked my neck and gazed up at the majestic walls of this ancient canyon. It seemed like those walls went up and up forever and ever, hundreds and in some places over two thousand feet! The deep red in the rocks and sheer cliffs began to have a powerful effect over me. As I walked around in utter astonishment, almost in a trance-like state, I began quietly singing the words to a beloved hymn that was sung at my grandpa's funeral, "How Great Thou Art."[34]

Oh Lord, my God
When I, in awesome wonder
Consider all the worlds Thy hands have made
I see the stars, I hear the rolling thunder
Thy power throughout the universe displayed

What I refer to as the Spirit of God overcame me as I beheld, in an all-encompassing manner, the grandeur of our great Creator. It hit me all at once: feelings, thoughts, a vision, a divine connection and experience so strong it was undeniable and would forever stay with me. It was as if the following message were being poured into every fiber of my being:

Andrew, these are rocks. Just rocks. You are my son! And
what you're feeling here, in the presence of my physical
creations, others can feel to an even greater extent when
you fulfill the measure of your spiritual creation. If I can bring
into being all of this beautiful landscape, I can certainly help
you create whatever I want and need, far superior than what
you're experiencing here in these canyons right now.

[34] Text: Stuart K. Hine, 1899–1989. *Author's original words are works and mighty.

Instantaneously, I knew I needed to do more than I was currently doing. I did need to write a book–this book–and from this moment on, I could no longer live small. I would accept invitations to speak publicly now without hesitation. My Life Mission, from my Heavenly Father, is to influence as many as possible to live a higher level of spiritual strength and joy. And, when I'm not influencing as many as possible, I'm being selfish. This I knew with greater clarity than ever before.

I also knew that I had absolutely no idea how all of this would unfold. What I did have was the *why* and the *what*. The idea of **"Strength of the Oak, Strength of the Willow"** came into mind. I stood there by the river feeling God's liberating presence and I just wept.

In that moment, where time stood still, I began to understand the sacred nature of Zion National Park. I'd never had an experience to create a neurological anchor in this location and had never quite understood why others spoke the way they did about this place. But now, I got it... and so much more.

What was revealed to me that day was beyond the magnificence of the geological wonders surrounding me, although it was awe-inspiring, in and of itself. I had received a revelation regarding me, *my* brilliance, *my* magnificence, *my* liberating personal power that could be available if I were to live into the integrity of *my* divine presence.

The great sage from ancient India, Patañjali, said, "When you are inspired by some great purpose, some extraordinary project, all your thoughts break their bonds: Your mind transcends limitations, your consciousness expands in every direction, and you find yourself in a new, great and wonderful world. Dormant forces, faculties and talents become alive, and you discover yourself to be a greater person by far than you ever dreamed yourself to be."[35]

That...is the power of *your* presence.

Journal Entry 🖉 *How would you currently describe the power of your presence? If you're struggling to see yourself as a ten-plus, why? What*

---

[35] https://www.drwaynedyer.com/

makes that so difficult? If you do see yourself in this revealing light, the utmost expression of your highest and best self, how did you get here? What has your journey of enlightenment looked like?

DROPPING EGO

"The ego is only an illusion, but a very influential one. Letting the ego-illusion become your identity can prevent you from knowing your true self. Ego, the false idea of believing that you are what you have or what you do, is a backwards way of assessing and living life."
—Wayne Dyer

The ego (your falsely-perceived identity) *is* an illusion, just as Wayne Dyer, one of the late greats in the field of self-development and spiritual growth, explained. But what exactly does that mean–your ego is an illusion? We're going to explore this a bit more.

I want you to pretend like we're in a room together and all of the doors and windows have been sealed shut, completely void of any light entering. And then, we turn off the lights. It would appear as if we were in total and complete darkness, right? I then light a small match in the far corner of the room, and immediately, what happens? The darkness dissipates and a faint light is again present.

In that moment, what power does the darkness have over the light? None! Darkness cannot chase away light. The only way for darkness to be present is for light to vanish. And the only way for light to vanish is to extinguish its source—the matchstick and/or the oxygen. There is no other way to extinguish light. And darkness can only exist in the absence of light. And if something only exists in the absence of something else, does it really exist in and of itself? No!

Darkness, therefore, is an illusion. It does not exist in and of itself.

The twelfth century Old French roots of the word *illusion* suggest "a mocking, deceit, deception."[36] That is exactly what your ego is. It is mocking your true identity. It is a slippery deception of your higher self. Ego is the original culprit and criminal mastermind of identity theft.

So, how do we catch it and prevent its further devastation?

Simple. We turn on the lights.

Just like the illusion of darkness cannot exist in light, the illusion of ego cannot exist in truth. So, how do we turn on the lights of truth? We connect to the Source. And how do we connect to the Source? We ask a simple question to any ego-based belief: "Is that true?" And then, we follow up (if necessary) with, "Is that 100% true?"

Let's put this into a context that we might all be familiar with. Let's say you lose your temper and say something potentially hurtful to a loved one. After doing so, you see shame shaking its ugly head at you and you hear its disgusted rebuke, "You are awful. How dare you? Do you have any idea how bad of a friend, father, sister, etc. you are? How could you say that?"

STOP!

Ask the simple question, "Is that true? Am I awful and worthless?" Hopefully your conscience replies, "No, that's not true. You are not awful and worthless." But, if your ego does win this shouting match and says, "Yes, you *are* awful and worthless!" then comes the follow-up question: "Is that 100% true? Am I 100% awful and worthless?" As you get quiet, you'll hear your infinite self calmly reassuring, "No, that's not 100% true. Sure, you did something that might be awful and yes, you need to own that and make it right. And of course, it's making you and others question your worth. And yet, that is *not* who you are."

If needed, a further discovery can be made as we ask, "Is that all that I think I am? Aren't I more than that? So, what am I that's not awful and worthless?" And that still, small voice from deep within, that Source, will reply with affirming words of love and support, "You are caring, dedicated, kind, loving…, etc."

---

[36] https://www.etymonline.com/word/illusion

You can then take this one step further by asking, "And beyond _____, (whatever you answered above, "caring") is that all that I am? How much more am I than that? I do know I am more than that, don't I?" Listen to your heart and believe what you hear. Truth won't lie.

You can repeat those questions easily with yourself in a simple, therapeutic or meditative way. Here they are again for your ease:

DROPPING EGO QUESTIONS

— Is that true? Am I _____?
— (If needed) Is that 100% true? Am I 100% _____?
— (If needed) Is that all that I think I am?
— Aren't I more than that?
— So, what am I that's not _____?
— And beyond _____ (the word elicited in the previous question), is that all that I am?
— How much more am I than that?
— I do know I'm more than that, don't I?
— If desired, keep repeating the above questions and then end with, How do I know?

As you engage your higher self, you will be reminded that you are far greater than your conditioned behaviors. We are not our labels!

Healthy parents wouldn't dare look at a toddler and say, "You are such a spoiled brat! We do everything for you! Here we all are waiting hand and foot on 'She Who Sits Upon the Throne.' You are so selfish. You never think of others, only yourself. What's wrong with you!? When are you going to start pulling your weight around here? All you do is mooch off us and demand that all your needs and wants are taken care of. You are the most impatient person in this home. You throw tantrums every time you don't get what you want. What a sad little human you are. You should be ashamed of yourself!"

Could a small child be portraying some of these behaviors? Of course. Does that define who he or she is as a human? No way. These are simply age-appropriate behaviors. And yet, if someone close were to affirm that these actions do indeed define this child, then there would be an ego formed around these qualities. And this child would, therefore, continue to live out a life of similar self-fulfilling habits of child-like behavior. There would undoubtedly follow a self-loathing of a misconstrued false identity. And that is a crime that we cannot afford to commit.

So, once we've practiced the ego dropping and busted the broken record, how do we build from there?

You feed your faith.

Journal Entry 🖊 How do you see yourself using these "Dropping Ego Questions?" When might you have been able to employ them in real life this past week? What would have been different for you had you used them in that scenario? What could you do to ensure you use them in the future when your ego is hanging on for dear life?

FEED YOUR FAITH

As many times as I've heard this story, and I'm sure you might have as well, it bears repeating. As legend goes, an old Cherokee is teaching his grandson about life. "A fight is going on inside me," he said to the boy. "It is a terrible fight and it is between two wolves. One is evil – he is anger, envy, sorrow, regret, greed, arrogance, self-pity, guilt, resentment, inferiority, lies, false pride, superiority and ego."

He continued, "The other is good – he is joy, peace, love, hope, serenity, humility, kindness, benevolence, empathy, generosity, truth, compassion and faith. The same fight is going on inside you – and inside every other person too."

The grandson thought about it for a minute and then asked his grandfather, "Which wolf will win?"

The old Cherokee simply replied, "The one you feed."[37]

A surefire way to keep your ego out of the picture is to feed your faith. When you feed your faith, your fears will starve to death. Where there is light, darkness cannot and will not be present. Faith in that loving Being who is inextricably interwoven with your spiritual DNA is powerful beyond measure. Its power surpasses all understanding and is more than enough to drown out competing voices of fictitious falsehoods.

Whether you're an oak or a willow, a peach or pine tree, if the dusty winds of mortality land an undesirable bunch of deadly nightshade berries, or a few poison ivy leaves amongst your branches, it's okay. You don't need to chop down the whole tree thinking you've become something you're not. Those fatal berries and itchy leaves *do not* determine your destiny. You are much more than your environment. You have a Life Mission grounding you to your Source. You have clarity on principles and values that guide every step of your earthly journey. You carry gratitude and joy in your soul that propel you well beyond what others might make you try to vainly believe about who you are.

These few words from the Persian poet Rumi speak volumes, "The art of knowing is knowing what to ignore."

Let's ignore the ego and feed our faith as we watch those fears fade dismally away into the nothingness from whence they were created.

Journal Entry 🖊 *What do you know you could be doing right now that would feed your faith on a consistent basis? Can you commit to that? What would happen if you did? Who will you be when you are free from ego and standing in the power of your presence? What will this do for our seemingly darkened world?*

---

[37]   https://www.interfaithpeaceproject.org/listening-with-the-ear-of-your-heart-spiritual-practice-group-at-our-antioch-center-volume-5/

CHAPTER TEN

The Power of Your Creation

"Knowing others is wisdom, knowing yourself is Enlightenment."
—Lao Tzu

Very little in life brings me greater joy than lifting the lid off of a brand-new box of crayons. Seeing those smooth, clean, perfectly formed tips, all neatly lined up and ready to go. . .I've got a huge grin on my face just thinking about them. Or how about opening a fresh container of Play-Doh? The smell of that soft and salty, brightly colored dough, unmarred by eager hands, just waiting to be formed into something is in itself magical. Think of all the wonder, the excitement and the possibilities, literally, at your fingertips.

What if we brought a similar child-like reverence and enthusiasm to the masterpiece in the making that we call LIFE? Think about it. What if each morning you woke up and approached the day like that fresh box of crayons, eager to turn a crisp, white piece of paper into something worthy of being hung proudly on the fridge? How about looking at life like that perfect little lump of dough, willing to be molded into a majestic treasure of your imagination?

LIFE HAS NO MEANING?

"Life has no meaning. Each of us has meaning
and we bring it to life. It is a waste to be asking
the question when you are the answer."
—Joseph Campbell

I recently sat down with a bright, young woman who beamed with potential and a desire to have and do more in her life. Natalie was the daughter of one of my clients, and I had agreed to work with her more as a mentor and friend than as a professional coach. As we conversed, I found that she struggled to break a pattern of inconsistent habits, which led to her feeling a lack of personal integrity. She had been beating herself up for years after setting high standards and expectations and often falling short. This brought an immense amount of disappointment, irritation and sadness. Natalie felt like she had missed the mark, not risen to what she could be and was wasting away her life.

After listening to how this all came to be, I explained some simple principles about her conditioning, the labels she carried, the beliefs she'd erroneously held on to and the freedom that awaited her on the other side of this life-sucking monster she'd been hosting.

Natalie then asked an all too frequent question I have become accustomed to, "What will motivate me when all this baggage, the limiting beliefs, the painful emotions are gone? I feel like everything would just be...blah."

I did my best to validate her concern and then shared, "You know, many people feel the same way you do. People who struggle with drugs, alcohol, sex, gambling, shopping, food, cutting, staying in abusive relationships or any self-deprecating vice, all wonder at some point or another, 'Who would I be without this?'"

What Natalie didn't yet know is that there is a perceived emptiness that is easily projected when thinking about the future absence of ego. It can be as frightening as letting go of labels, maybe worse. And just like a black hole, we might fear what's inside and beyond that unknown. The best part about it is that this void does not exist. There is no meaning to life or this empty space. As Joseph Campbell said, "We are the meaning." In fact, I know that we are big enough to fill any vacuum created from the destruction of a false self. We are full of a light that easily fills the immensity of space. This light is in all things and gives life to all things. Its powerful abundance governs and brings order to the Universe.

I explained to Natalie that as soon as we got done eliminating these limiting beliefs and the negative emotions that had been working against her for the entirety of her life, she would enjoy a relief and bliss beyond anything she'd ever experienced before. She looked at me with some serious skepticism, which is normal. I'm used to it.

At this point an analogy often helps. Let's imagine we live in one of the poorest countries in the world, Burundi, located in East Africa. We are used to a diet of one meal a day consisting of either corn, millet, sorghum, cassava or, if we're lucky, sweet potatoes or maybe even beans. One day, I look at you and say, "Hey, guess what!? We're going to begin eating three meals a day, some snacks in between, and we're going to cap it all off with the most delicious dessert known to mankind---ice cream!" And yet, even as I share my description of this delectably sweet, smooth and creamy frozen delicacy, you might be 100% lost and in so much pain of hunger that you have zero interest in my food fantasy. It's beyond your comprehension.

A lot of people are in such mental, emotional and spiritual starvation that they have an extremely hard time imagining what could possibly be on the other side of it. And what they end up finding is this blank recipe card, ready to be filled with their unique ingredients to create a new and exciting ice cream the world has never known.

Life, like that recipe card, is a blank slate. It has no meaning, except what we bring to it. And that is always our choice. The degree to which one feels empowered in making that choice is the degree to which one is able to see past any ego and into their higher self.

The biblical Apostle Paul, having gone through his own powerful conversion and then dedicating the remainder of his life to helping others do the same, taught, "For now we see through a glass [mirror], darkly; but then face to face: now I know in part; but then shall I know even as also I am known" (1 Corinthians 13:12). At one point he referred to this kind of knowing as "the mind of Christ" (1 Corinthians 2:16).

Each and every one of us--although maybe not until after this life--will see with absolute clarity who we are. We will know as we are known with the precise understanding of our Eternal Parents. And I declare, with all my heart-felt passion, that we do not have to wait until death brings us past the bonds of mortality to have this kind of awakening. We can know NOW and live in alignment TODAY with who and what we truly mean for this world.

All we need is some clarity. Like a couple squirts of windshield wiper fluid and a few back-and-forth motions of the blades, we all deserve to be able to see the beautiful vistas ahead and the strength that lies within.

CLARITY IS POWER

*"Feel yourself grounded to the earth, while your
mind is focusing on the sky of clarity."*
—Nawang Kechog

An architect takes a look at a clear skyline or open horizon and envisions something gracing that space that does not yet exist. It is the clarity and freedom to build, to design, to construct and to create that moves the architect to produce a piece of art that surpasses functionality.

One of the masters and major figures in architecture of the late twentieth and early twenty-first centuries was Zaha Habid. She explained that, "Architecture is really about well-being. I think that people want to feel good in a space...On the one hand it's about shelter, but it's also about pleasure."[38]

I love that! The similarities between designing buildings, and our lives, run in a beautifully parallel path.

Our lives hold space. They are a shelter for our soul. Safety from outside influences is of utmost concern. And if that's all life was about--surviving--then we'd experience some awfully sad mortal existences. Life truly is about well-being, feeling good in our space and pleasure. This is not the fleeting pleasure that promises all in

---

[38] https://www.vogue.com.au/vogue-living/design/zaha-hadids-most-memorable-and-inspiring-quotes/image-gallery/b92978d33fc292acc66edd1945b2d1bc

the moment and leaves us empty and worse off when it's gone. This is the pleasure that adds spice to the main course, the cherry on top, the adorning garnish.

Clarity is the reward for dropping ego, being grounded in a Life Mission and having values and principles to pull us through anything. It's knowing what's waiting deep inside you, ready and eager to be revealed for the world. It's the power of your presence as you move forward in a state of gratitude, joy, focus and commitment, having turned your life over to God.

Possessing the gift of clarity means you are now ready to put all of this together into a master blueprint. We're going to build a powerful theme park for your life, one that will have you and others sitting in awe, wondering how in the world you got so lucky. It will grace the open air of your life in a jaw-dropping, "take my breath away" kind of experience that you're never going to want to leave!

PLAYING TO WIN

I can't tell you how many times I've heard my dad say, "You've gotta play to win! Don't play not to lose!" Nothing irks him more than watching a good team try to run out the clock at the end of the game. His knee starts bouncing up and down and he might even get the back and forth, full-body rocking motion going. This means he's nervous! "Just do what you've been doing all game. Score! Play to win! Shoot the ball! Go for the end zone! Swing for the bleachers!"

This was ingrained in me growing up. I swung at everything playing Little League baseball. Going down watching a ball go by was unacceptable! I struck out a lot because of this, but you'd hardly ever see me watching a strike whiz past without swinging.

Whether it was Sun Tzu, George Washington or Knute Rockne who first coined the phrase, the message is what matters most: *The best defense is a good offense.*

I've seen this time and time again throughout my life in many arenas outside of athletics. The most memorable would have to be what has come to be known as "The Rat Park."

In the 1970s, American psychologist, Dr. Bruce Alexander,[39] conducted an experiment with, you guessed it, rats! Scientists had already proven that when placed in a cage or maze in total isolation, rats would repeatedly drink from drug-laced water bottles over normal water bottles. They would continue to do so until they all overdosed and died from the heroin or cocaine.

Dr. Alexander was brewing up a new hypothesis. He wondered if the previous outcomes were more correlated to the drugs or the environment that the rats found themselves in. Putting his hypothesis to the test, he created Rat Parks, where these furry experimentees were offered everything they could ever need and want and more! They were placed in a spacious, cageless, maze-less area where they were free to roam and play. Spinning wheels, tunnels and ladders allowed for exercise. Fruit, plants, seeds and cheese were offered in an unmatched buffet fit for rodent royalty. And friends! Other rats were introduced, creating a community of socialization and sex.

The result? Given equal access to the same two types of water bottles--drug laced and normal--the rats remarkably preferred the plain water. The drug-filled bottles were only intermittently tasted, almost from a place of curiosity, not obsessively and to everyone's surprise, never to the point of overdose. The physical and social environment won out over the addictive drugs.

When I first heard of this phenomenon, my mind went directly to the world I know best, not drug rehab centers or prisons, but everyday life. I thought about how many people, including myself at times, seek relief from pain in harmful vices rather than building our environments. We have been conditioned to play defense, to play not to lose, and we have thrown out any offensive game plans.

---

[39] Alexander, Bruce K. (2010). Addiction: The View from Rat Park. Available from http://www.brucekalexander.com/articlesspeeches/rat-park/148-addiction-the-view-from-rat-park

Think of it...your own Rat Park, a life filled with all you need, want and more! One client of mine decided to call hers "Michelle's Magic Kingdom," a much more alluring name than Michelle's Rat Park! Regardless of what you call it, designing a life, playing offense, being so intentional with your environment that there's no room for mediocrity and disappointment, is a winning game plan.

Let's do this! Time to build.

> *"I only hope that we don't lose sight of one thing – that it was all started by a mouse."*
> —Walt Disney

YOUR RAT PARK

> *"The desire to create is one of the deepest yearnings of the human soul."*
> — Dieter F. Uchtdorf

This is going to take some serious brain power, and I know it's in you. You are more than a simple primate with opposable thumbs. Your brain is about three times larger and contains twice as many cells as your closest competitor, the chimpanzee. You've got this!

Now that I've built you up, I want you to imagine that you are nearing the end of your sensational sojourn here on Earth. You have an opportunity at this well-matured age to look back, with 20/20 hindsight, and see some things that maybe you've never considered in such an all-encompassing, panoramic picture.

#1 BE

As you look back on your life, what words would you use to describe who you've become over the years? What characteristics have you developed? How do others refer to you? What do you believe are the qualities that you will be remembered for? What do those who love you most and know you best say about your personality and your nature? Who have you become?

_____

_____

_____

_____

_____

#2 DO

What have you accomplished throughout your life? What did you do? Where did you go? Who did you serve? What kind of work were you passionate about? What was your impact on your family, friends, community, humanity? What skills did you acquire or master? What habits did you form? What talents did you develop and share? What special relationships did you cultivate? What did your life look like in action?

_____

_____

_____

_____

_____

#3 HAVE

What do you now have or did you have at one point? Did you finish that coin collection that meant so much to your grandfather? Did you

THE POWER OF YOUR CREATION

take care of your mother's hand-crafted quilts? Did you finally restore your father's classic car? Did you share family memories in a vacation home, on a boat or in an RV? What did you have in your life that meant the world to you? What relationships do you have that are priceless? Think materially, relationally, spiritually. What gifts do you have or did you have at one time or another that you treasure? What have you acquired that is invaluable to you?

_____

_____

_____

_____

_____

As you answer these questions, think holistically, all aspects of your life. Include everything that comes to your mind. Leave nothing out. Don't judge it. If it surfaces, put it down. We can come back through with a fine-toothed comb later. This is a brainstorming session. Leave judgment behind.

Once you have an initial list, go back through the questions again and allow yourself to dream beyond limitations. This is your life that you're reviewing. What would you see if you knew it was impossible to fail between now and the joyful end? Who are you? What have you done? And what do you have or what have you been able to give away through the years?

One last time, look over those questions, please. If there was just one or two more things you'd like to add to each of those lists, what would they be? Think BIG! This is your theme park called life and there's no cap to the creative possibilities that will lead to your amusement. You get to stand proud at the end of your life with as much peace of mind and gratification as Walt Disney might have experienced when he said, "*I dream, I test my dreams against my beliefs, I dare to take*

121

risks and I execute my vision to make those dreams come true."

As you look over your mental or first creation, I invite you to ask, "Does this vision hold joy? Would I be able to pass from this life with peace of conscience being, doing and having what I've envisioned?" If the answer is a resounding, 'Yes!' then you're done. If there's still some work to do, keep going. You have all the time in the world to add to this and expand it. And while perfect is great, done is better. So, let's move on with what you do have and continue to build as we go.

SEE IT

> *"Float like a butterfly sting like a bee – his*
> *hands can't hit what his eyes can't see."*
> —*Muhammad Ali*

The surest way to hit a goal is to first know that you can see it. The most self-actualizing and goal-attaining people do all they can to surround their physical environment with reminders of the life they are building. They create a vision board for the BE, DO and HAVE answers we've uncovered above. And you can do the same.

Go to the Internet and copy and paste images that represent everything you have in mind. You could also go to magazines and physically cut and paste. It doesn't matter how you do it, what matters is that it's done. Your vision board could be on a small note card all the way up to a wall-sized banner, or anywhere in between. The point is that you have a visual trigger to stimulate the neural pathways that were created when you set this dream deep in your unconscious mind when you answered those questions above.

Make sure every word and idea are visually represented in this graphic. What we focus on expands and we want to make sure we get it all. Find a place to keep your vision board that will remind you, several times a day, what matters most. This is, essentially, the blueprint for your Rat Park.

PRIORITIZE IT

Just as a contractor will not start working on the wiring until the framing is complete or the framing until the foundation is laid, there is wisdom in bringing order to the priorities and timing of the life we're building.

Benjamin Franklin said, "Lost time is never found again."[40] I've also heard a few different renditions of the idea that we often overestimate what we can do in one year and underestimate what we can do in five or ten. Certainly, we could all bring greater intentionality to the time we've been gifted.

As you look at this Rat Park, this life by design, ask yourself:

- Of all these things, what do I desire most and when?
- Would I regret not achieving this sooner?
- Might I regret having put so much energy toward this early in my life when I could have been present elsewhere and waited until later?
- Is this most desirable now, in one year, two-three years, five years, ten years, twenty years, etc.?

As you map out a timeline for what you want most for your life, you gain a purpose that propels you forward *now*. Having a prioritized path empowers us so that we do not have to exert great mental energy in making day-to-day and moment-to-moment decisions. When the choice for our future has been made, you know what to do right now. No messing around. **Strength of the Oak.**

RESOURCE IT—COUNT THE COST

Once we've mapped out what this Rat Park is going to look like and when, exactly, we'll be enjoying each phase, we now want to consider

---

[40] Poor Richard's Almanack, 1747 https://www.fi.edu/benjamin-franklin/famous-quotes.

the resources needed to build what we've envisioned.

Let's say, under the "HAVE" section, you wrote down: *In thirty years, I will own an island.* That's thinking big and I love it! Do you know what it takes to own an island? How much money will it cost? What are islands selling for today? Do you know anyone that has ever purchased one? What did they have to do to make this happen?

Or maybe under the "BE" section, you wrote down: *In five years, I will be a person of 100% integrity.* There's an attribute worth striving for! What does it take to become that kind of a person? Where are you now? What's the gap? What qualities does someone of 100% integrity also possess? Who do you know that's a great model of this? How did they get there? What will this journey look like for you?

These are examples of questions that will help you gather resources as you move toward each aspect of your life by design.

I'm sure you can see the train of thought that could go into this kind of resourcing. And this is an important part of the process. I see so many people who go through life, making goals and commitments, and never achieving what they desire because they didn't count the cost. And when they fail to hit their goals, they think they're not worthy enough or just don't have what it takes. Then, they often form an aversion to "goal setting" or other methods of creating a life worth living. How sad!

Jesus, the Great Carpenter, He who knows better than any what it takes to build a life by design, shared this wise analogy found in the gospel of Luke, "For which of you, intending to build a tower, sitteth not down first, and counteth the cost, whether he have sufficient to finish it? Lest haply, after he hath laid the foundation, and is not able to finish it, all that behold it begin to mock him, saying, 'This man began to build, and was not able to finish'" (Luke 14:28-30).

Counting the cost is worth every second we can devote to it. It is an easily forgotten or sometimes unknowingly missed step. I urge you to take the time necessary to consider the resources needed as you bring this blueprint to fruition. It will be more than worth the time and energy allotted. I promise.

IMPLEMENT IT

> *"Good thoughts are no better than good*
> *dreams if you don't follow through."*
> —*Ralph Waldo Emerson*

If you've come this far in the book, I know one thing for certain, you *want* this Rat Park, this co-created life by design that is *so* good, you'd never go to anything or anyone else for a false pledge of temporary happiness.

That desire, that want, that drive is in you. It's an intrinsic pull toward your best version of you. David A. Bednar said, "Nothing outside of you makes you move for any sustained period of time. The only thing that will cause you to move is what's inside...the only motivation that matters comes from within and is a function of seeing what we really are."[41]

That motivation is the number one ingredient in what I have termed, "The Rule of 3". The Rule of 3 consists of three simple keys that always seem to be present when success is in the air. And when goals aren't met and healthy habits are not formed, one or more of the 3 invariably seems to be missing.

The Rule of 3

1. **Internal Motivation (Do you really want it?)**
2. **System (Is there a system in place that is nearly fail-proof?)**
3. **Accountability (Who will best hold you accountable to this outcome?)**

I know you've got the internal motivation or you wouldn't still be reading. Let's talk systems and implementation now.

Time and time again, a client will say something to me like, "I just

---

[41] "A Conversation on Leadership"
February 24, 2010 http://broadcast.lds.org/elearning/hrd/LDSLeader/RESOURCES/Bednar_Script_no%20timecodes[1].pdf

don't know if I'm motivated enough to get this done." I respond with, "What's the system, the process you have in place, to guarantee your successful completion of this endeavor?" Their response never ceases to amaze me, "Umm...I don't really have one," or "It's not very good."

Here they are, beating themselves up on motivation when they just don't have a working system or process in place. This can save you so much unneeded heartache!

Let's take this one, for example, a client says, "You know, I really want to read more."

I love this goal! Readers are leaders and learners are earners! And yet, it's not quite specific enough, nor is it measurable. To make sure that the intrinsic motivation is there I'll ask, "Do you really want this? Why? Sell me on it." If I'm convinced, I come back to specificity and measurability. If it's not specific and measurable, we're just heading in a general, undetermined direction, only to "read more." This could be accomplished by simply reading the billboards you pass driving down the road or taking in the advertisements in the restaurant bathrooms. And I'm guessing this isn't exactly the end we had in mind.

So, we create a system that can easily be reproduced. You could hand this over to almost anyone and they'd be able to knock it down.

"I will read for at least fifteen minutes, somewhere between 9:00 p.m. and 10:00 p.m., M-F, in my bed, with an alarm on my phone at 9:45 p.m. asking, 'How was reading?' I will start with this specific book and then ask my work colleagues for recommendations on the next best read."

Now we're talking!

How about another example, "I want to have a net worth of $1M."

Great goal! Net worth is an essential indicator of wealth. And yet, it's still not quite specific enough, nor measurable.

"I will have a net worth of $1M in at least ten years. This will consist of adding X amount of dollars each month to my retirement/saving account, I will have paid off my primary residence, I will have X number of dollars in these liquid assets, and will do so by earning this amount of money in year one, and this amount in year two, and so forth."

There's a system!

My father's words, echoing through the corridors of time all the way back to being a twelve-year-old Boy Scout, continue to ring true, "If we fail to plan, we plan to fail." I learned to do hard things during those seven years of scouting. Having my dad as the Scoutmaster for two of them ensured that these were *really* hard things.

There's a photograph that resurfaces from time to time when visiting my parents' home. There I was, as a thirteen-year-old, straddling a fallen tree, about two feet in diameter, with me sporting the nastiest grimace you've ever seen. *"Why in the world are you taking a picture right now?"* is precisely what that face says. I was suspended nearly ten feet above the icy cold, snow-covered Crooked River in Idaho. Slipping and sliding in front of me was Zach, a fellow scouter who was just as annoyed, or maybe more so; he had Air Jordan's on and didn't want to watch them wash away into the wintery waters below.

For some reason unbeknownst to me, this seemed like the best way to cross that freezing death trap. We were literally knocking off tree limbs with a hatchet so as to "safely" scoot across this soon-to-be man-made bridge. I don't know what boyhood emotion was greater, being terrified or ticked off.

Somehow, with what I'm guessing must have been angelic help from the other side, all eight boys and three adult leaders miraculously made it to the other side of that unnerving body of water. Thinking back, I almost wonder if my dad specifically selected that spot to cross, knowing there was another, easier way, and betting (our lives!) that this one would be much more memorable, and character building.

Two lessons from that ten-mile snowy hike (yes, I verified with my old man, the Scoutmaster, it was indeed ten miles and the snow was up to our knees in certain places):

Lesson #1: The Scout Motto: Be prepared. Who thinks of bringing a hatchet on a hike?

Lesson #2: Air Jordans look pretty cool on the court, and they are terrible for winter hikes. Thanks for the lesson, Zach. . .

"If we fail to plan, we plan to fail."

Implementation is simple, and a heck of a lot easier, when we know we really want it *and* have the right shoes and tools, a well-prepared system or process in place to ensure its success.

Dr. Orison Swett Marden, inspirational author and founder of *SUCCESS* magazine stated, "A good system shortens the road to the goal." I'll take a good system over a fallen tree any day! And, there's more...the third and culminating piece of the puzzle in the Rule of 3: Accountability. This one might actually be the cheat code to success, leading us up and on to a whole new level.

Let's go.

CHAPTER ELEVEN

The Champion's Plane

"A body of men holding themselves accountable to nobody ought not to be trusted by anybody."
—Thomas Paine

A friend recently said to me, "I just feel like if I have to have someone hold me accountable then I'm just not motivated enough. I shouldn't need a babysitter."

I replied, "Tell that to the world's most elite athletes who hire personal trainers, nutritionists and mindset coaches. What do you think they understand about accountability that we too can learn from?"

"Good point."

Accountability is a sign of strength, **Strength of the Willow**. It means we're not so hard-headed and high-minded that we can't accept the humbling power of vulnerability that comes from admitting we have failed our way forward. It shows we're open to feedback on how to be *better*. In fact, there is no failure, only feedback. And if feedback is the fastest way to fortune and success, then the more the merrier!

When it comes to accountability, our central nervous system is a masterful model of feedback at its finest. Check it out...

Let's say you touch a burning pan that has just come out of the oven, which you were not aware of before you touched it. The nervous tissue in your skin is made up of millions of neurons that carry the heavy responsibility of transmitting messages through cells that connect all the way up to your brain. This message is traveling at the speed of more than three hundred feet per second. Your brain receives the alarming message and shoots one back, just as fast, telling your muscles to pull your hand away–ASAP![42]

This is what we call a feedback loop, a biological mechanism that brings the bodily system closer to a target of stability or homeostasis. The mind-blowing miracle to me is that this is constantly happening amongst the thirty trillion cells in our body. Thirty trillion! To put that in perspective, there are as many cells in your body as people on this earth...times 3,800! Think of each cell representing a tiny communicating person inside you and there are as many people inside you as 3,800 Earths populated like ours!!![43]

And it actually works. And you're sitting there thinking, "I have a hard time just communicating and maintaining homeostasis with one human being!"

Thirty trillion!

What's the lesson on feedback for us here? If the most stunning creation on this planet, the human body, is composed of a fine-tuned, multi-layered and multi-dimensional feedback system, maybe we should consider building one into the *life* we're creating as well.

Here are some simple, and fun, examples I've seen over the years where accountability made all the difference:

1. **Kayla**: After almost ten years in a 100% commission, sales-based, independent contractor career, Kara had not yet built a database of past clients with whom she could stay in touch and receive referrals. She knew she was missing out on a lot of business because she simply hadn't built a platform to help her keep up with these relationships. She chose a painful consequence to help her stay accountable to the goal she'd set to build this database. If she didn't have every name, phone number, mailing and email address in that system in ninety days, she would have to send a $1,000.00 check to her previous boss who had told her that when she left that organization, she'd never make it on her own. When

---

[42] https://www.britannica.com/science/axon
[43] https://www.healthline.com/health/number-of-cells-in-body

the ninety days were up and the database was complete, she destroyed that check. Victory.

2. **Marie** knew she wasn't an alcoholic, and yet felt compelled to drink less in hopes of finding greater health and self-control in the process. She had a close friend across the country who, at the same time, wanted help with eating much healthier. These two created a simple electronic tracking system to help hold each other accountable in achieving their goals. Their desire to support one another and not let each other down created a friendly way for them to each find the success they were looking for, hand in hand.

3. **Rick** was an avid bowhunter and had never purchased the crown jewel of bows that he'd always had his eye on. He knew that this reward would be more than enough to motivate him to show up and produce in his business and meet the financial goals he had for him and his family. I still remember the day he sent me a picture of that bow. It was beautiful to behold.

4. **Stephanie**: Children are some of the greatest accountability partners in the world! You promise them something and they never forget it! Stephanie had three kids who had been begging her to go to Disneyland for years. She made a deal with them that when she reached her sales goals, their Disney dream would come true. She got to hear, "Mom, did you sell a house today?" hundreds of times that year as they tracked her progress on the refrigerator. That was a memorable trip, and year, for the whole family.

5. **Jess** was a competitor to the core. Winning was the only option if she ever chose to play a game or enter a competition. So, when it came to her physical fitness and nutrition goals, she loved joining social network communities where everyone had some stakes involved. She knew if she entered, her health goals would be guaranteed. I loved that smile whenever she shared with me what she'd recently won. Good pride, well-earned in her competition with herself.

There are so many different ways to put some scaffolding of accountability into our lives. Competitions, rewards, accountability teams and partners, negative consequences, tracking systems, calendars, challenges, deadlines and so many more. The important thing is that you have someone or something or both that allows you to monitor your progress.

> *"When performance is measured, performance improves. When performance is measured and reported back, the rate of improvement accelerates."*
> —*Thomas Monson*

DOOR HINGES

The Rule of 3 is like hinges on a door. One is good, two are better, and three is best. If you want to ensure longevity and ease when it comes to using that door, include all three hinges. And so it is with what we want most out of our life goals. If you want to witness success that lasts and an ease of flow rather than force, make sure you've got all three:

1. The internal motivation to pull you forward.
2. A sure-fire system to follow.
3. The accountability to keep you on track.

With all three of these hinges in place, you can gracefully open and close that door, having the confidence you need to come and go as you please. Your dreams and passions are waiting for you. Open the dang door!

INSPECT WHAT YOU EXPECT

"The purpose of a goal is to be appropriate in the moment."
—Gary Keller

As we bring attention and awareness to where we are compared to where we have planned to be, we can know if our here and now is appropriate or not. An extremely effective approach is to adopt the old adage to "inspect what we expect."

Let me share a surefire system with you which, when implemented effectively, becomes an absolute game changer for your productivity and overall happiness. I'm giving you a tool that I use with my clients to ensure your motivation, system and personal accountability are in place. My recommendation is that you engage the help of a quality professional (like a coach), a friend or a supportive partner whenever possible. Here's how it works:

Once a week, block some time in your calendar for what we'll call a "411 Meeting" (Gratitude to Keller Williams for teaching this one to me.). This time will become as valuable to you as anything you could do the rest of the week. The purpose of this meeting is for you to make certain that each moment of the coming month and week is appropriately aligned with the vision you hold of your ideally executed plans. You can do this individually for your personal life or job, with a business partner or anyone else who shares ownership of outcomes that are important to you, like a significant other. Share it with whomever you've asked to hold you accountable.

Take a look at this example of a 4-1-1 Worksheet I use with all of my clients:

4-1-1 WORKSHEET

ANNUAL GOALS | YEAR

MONTHLY GOALS | MONTH OF

WEEKLY GOALS

WEEK 1	WEEK 2	WEEK 3	WEEK 4

The "4" stands for four weeks in a month. The "1" is one month of goals. And the last "1" is for one year of goals. This is a sample form that you can use during your weekly 411 Meeting. You're going to use one form per month.

As a new month approaches, you write out, as a reminder, what your most important goals are for the year. Yes, you will be writing these yearly goals twelve times, but repetition is indeed the mother of all learning…and skill sets! You'll also write out what you plan to accomplish for this new month. Think big rocks, 20%, the most important and urgent goals you'll reach this month that, once met, will ensure you're well on your way to celebrating the achievement of your yearly goals. Each week you'll write out what must be executed this week for you to be on track for your monthly goals.

Take it one step further and open up your calendar. Think of your schedule as a budget for your goals. Block time for the coming week so your weekly goals show up as priorities on your calendar. "If it's not on your schedule, it doesn't exist" (kwMAPS Coaching, BOLD Laws).

Each week as you hold your 411 Meeting, you'll be able to go back and see how well you showed up for your ideal week. You may take some things that didn't happen last week and move them to this next week. This is a critical pause… for you to work ON your life rather than constantly being IN it. It's a time out, a huddle, a breather. You get to regroup, and get your head, heart and calendar right for what's to come.

As a new month approaches, you pull out a new sheet, write down your yearly goals, determine what you'll accomplish for the month and get that first week mapped out. Rinse, repeat.

I've seen a lot of ways that people have succeeded with this tool. Some have stapled twelve sheets together for the year, others make a notebook or binder out of it. I've seen this implemented electronically on a computer or device. Whatever works for you, go with it!

Like a vehicle, its main purpose is to get you from Point A to Point B. Comfort and style can come later. The only way to fail epically is to not do it at all.

I invite you to look at your calendar right now and select a day and time to hold this meeting. Start with fifteen-thirty minutes. I'm sure you'll get to the point, eventually, where you'll be able to do this in less time, and for now, let's make sure you're not rushed.

What day? Totally up to you. What I've found with my clients is that Monday morning is too late! You don't want to wake up and start the week without a plan. Sunday night is also cutting it pretty close. Sometimes we have fun things going on that night or we're recovering from the weekend and it's hard to put the mental energy toward planning. Anywhere from Friday morning through Sunday afternoon often works best. I do understand that you might have a wonky work or personal schedule and you'll be better off doing it on a weekday. Simply find what works best for you and adjust as needed.

The capstone to the 411 process is a quick end-of-day wrap up, or as I like to call it, Calendar Calibration. It's a simple way to turn one day off and plan for the next. Let me explain.

As you wind down your day, it's tempting to dismiss tomorrow. Don't do it! Stop and take two minutes before you move on, pull out your 411 and review the blocked time on your calendar that you already scheduled during your weekly 411 Meeting. Is there anything that has taken a higher place of priority and urgency that needs to be accounted for tomorrow? If so, remember this: If you erase, you must replace! Think of your goals for the week as money you owe yourself. If you push it off, the debt doesn't just go away. You still owe it to yourself. So, when will you reschedule that commitment that's getting bumped today?

This is a moment of truth. Will you or will you not keep your word to yourself? We cannot show up for others better than we show up for ourselves. You deserve the absolute most trusting relationship with you that is possible. You're stuck with that reflection in the mirror for the entirety of your life. And if you don't like what you see inside, there's no separation or breaking up or divorce. So, let's get real. Eliminate excuses. Hand deliver to yourself the gift of integrity that you are entitled to as one of your human rights.

This 411 Meeting and daily Calendar Calibration is a **Strength of the Oak** system. Giving yourself permission to adjust and shift as needed is **Strength of the Willow**, self-grace. Recommitting to what must be moved on the calendar and not letting it fall through the cracks, **Strength of the Oak**. I trust you are beginning to see a vital pattern.

As you continue to hold strong to your plans *and* go with the flow, you'll be managing essential energy in a brilliantly orchestrated way. When your mental and emotional energy are contained like this, you won't have to waste it on wondering what to do next or now. The decision has been made! You can use that conserved energy to create something new, a beautiful life by design!

Journal Entry 🖊 *I commit to holding a weekly 411 Meeting each _____ at __:__*

SWING STATE–THE CHAMPION'S PLANE

> *"It's a great art, is rowing. It's the finest art there is. It's a symphony of motion. And when you're rowing well, why it's nearing perfection. And when you near perfection, you're touching the Divine. It touches the you of yous. Which is your soul."*
> —George Yeoman Pocock

I couldn't put it down. *The Boys in the Boat: Nine Americans and Their Epic Quest for Gold at the 1936 Berlin Olympics*, a nonfiction novel written by Daniel James Brown, had my heart and mind reeling for days, which turned into weeks and months. This heroic story introduced me to a world I previously knew nothing about--rowing--and a powerful principle I have come to cherish, "swing."

George Yeoman Pocock was known around the globe for designing and building, by hand, the absolute finest and fastest racing shells (boats) in the world of rowing, or crew racing as it's called in America. Pocock's shells would lead the USA to Olympic gold medals in Eight Oar Rowing in 1936, 1948, 1952, 1956, 1960 and 1964.

Nobody knew the intricate relationship between a boat and a crew better than George Yeoman Pocock. He not only handcrafted each of those gold medal shells, he played an intimate role in the boys and men who were privileged enough to row these magnificent creations.

Pocock knew that, "A good shell has to have life and resiliency to get in harmony with the swing of the crew."[44] And yet, the shell doesn't get there alone. The crew has to show up. "When you get the rhythm in an eight [eight-man boat], it's pure pleasure to be in it. It's not hard work when the rhythm comes—that 'swing' as they call it. I've heard men shriek out with delight when that swing came in an eight; it's a thing they'll never forget as long as they live."[45]

This *swing*. It's nearly impossible to achieve and just as difficult to describe. Most, and even the best, never get close to finding it. And if it is found, good luck holding on to it!

Brown goes on to describe it beautifully:

It only happens when all eight oarsmen are rowing in such perfect unison that no single action by any one is out of sync with those of all the others.

He goes on to describe what he means by a team working in sync with each other:

Sixteen arms must begin to pull, sixteen knees must begin to fold and unfold, eight bodies must begin to slide forward and

---

[44] Brown, Daniel James. The Boys in the Boat: Nine Americans and Their Epic Quest for Gold at the 1936 Berlin Olympics. United States, Penguin Publishing Group, 2021, p. 169.
[45] Brown, Daniel James. The Boys in the Boat: Nine Americans and Their Epic Quest for Gold at the 1936 Berlin Olympics. United States, Penguin Publishing Group, 2021, p. 305.

backward, eight backs must bend and straighten all at once. Each minute action—each subtle turning of wrists—must be mirrored exactly by each oarsman, from one end of the boat to the other. Only then will the boat continue to run, unchecked, fluidly and gracefully between pulls of the oars.[46]

This idyllic state of poetic harmony brings body and boat together; there's no distinction between either. When swing is achieved, any thought of pain disappears as exultation takes over. Maintaining this steady flow becomes increasingly difficult as the tempo increases, until it's practically inconceivable. But, as Brown so masterfully explains, "the closer a crew can come to that ideal—maintaining a good swing while rowing at a high rate—the closer they are to rowing on another plane, the plane on which champions row."[47]

"The plane on which champions row," those words!

As a coach, when I hear something like that, there's an immediate and electric kind of shiver that jolts up and down my spine, bringing a mile-wide smile from ear to ear. It makes me want to explode out of my seat, arms and hands fist pumping into the air and throw myself into a celebratory hug with an imaginary teammate in absolute elation! That's the stuff that ignites the deepest kinds of fire in my bones!

I recall with vivid detail the end of an early morning mountain bike ride as I flew down the trail with the crisp, fall air in my face. I was listening to the audio recording of Mr. Brown detailing what happens in this magical swing state attained by eight men in a shell. Right away, I decided to teach this powerful new principle to a group I would be speaking in front of that very morning. They were on a team retreat, gaining perspective, setting goals and creating individual and business plans for the following year. I was invited to come in as a keynote speaker to share something inspiring to kick off their retreat.

---

[46] Brown, Daniel James. The Boys in the Boat: Nine Americans and Their Epic Quest for Gold at the 1936 Berlin Olympics. United States, Penguin Publishing Group, 2021, p.216.
[47] Brown, Daniel James. The Boys in the Boat: Nine Americans and Their Epic Quest for Gold at the 1936 Berlin Olympics. United States, Penguin Publishing Group, 2021, p.217

I couldn't shake this new-found knowledge and feeling of such a powerful principle. I explained to them that before any team steps into a boat, a business, a relationship or any interdependent environment, swing should always be the ideal outcome for which we strive. And if we expect to reach this together, how can we ever hope to do so if we do not find swing in our individual lives?

"Harmony, balance, and rhythm. They're the three things that stay with you your whole life. Without them civilization is out of whack. And that's why an oarsman, when he goes out in life, he can fight it, he can handle life. That's what he gets from rowing."
—George Yeoman Pocock

Having never set foot in a racing shell, I still somehow feel the sentiment of what Pocock and Brown are striving to get across. I feel it because I know personally what it's like when swing is not present in my life. I've dealt with forcing, gritting, grinding and failing my way forward in a manner that exerts way too much energy and leaves me gasping, hurting and wondering, "Isn't there an easier way."

The answer is a resounding 'YES!'

Let me share a story as to how I personally discovered this swing, painfully.

$1000 AND THE GOLDEN GOOSE

Somehow my iPhone found itself sandwiched between my hand and the granite countertop in my kitchen. The two happened to meet on impact at a high velocity with a great deal of force behind it. It was the tail end of what I have now labeled our "$1,000 fight."

I had gotten upset over something worth way less than $1000. We were planning a weekend getaway with Chari's family to one of my favorite places on the entire planet, McCall, Idaho. It's the most beautiful, serene and quaint all-American lake and ski town. I have the most amazing memories of vacationing there with cousins as a child, snow skiing with family friends, Boy Scout Camp for an entire week during three different summers of the best years of boyhood and now this new tradition of taking our family and hers to a place we cherish.

In arranging our lodging, I was set on the idea of having a few of the teenage kids and young adults sleep on air mattresses, couches and futons. Chari wanted each person to enjoy the luxury of having their own bed, which to me meant more bedrooms, a bigger cabin, and (this is me NOT being abundant) more money. We were clearly at odds over the decision. I was sure that I was right and was unyielding in my position. *Spoiled–that's what all these youngsters are these days! When I was a kid…*

The phone was just one victim of my vile pride, as it cracked, shattered and splintered enough under my pressure that it no longer had the capacity to properly function. It was done for, beyond reviving, hopelessly…dead.

The next morning, I called my good friend and mentor, Kevin Hall, and shared what had happened, yearning for some advice and perspective. He then proceeded to share with me one of Aesop's famous fables for children. I was, admittedly, being childish, so I listened intently:

Once upon a time a poor countryman possessed a most wonderful prized goose. Each day, as he visited its nest, he'd find that the goose "had laid a beautiful, glittering, golden egg." The countryman took his golden eggs to the market and quickly became quite rich. However, it didn't take long before he grew impatient with his precious goose, for she gave him but one solitary, single egg per day. His wealth was not growing fast enough for his selfish heart.

A stroke of genius entered his mind after counting his money one day. *I could get all the golden eggs at once if I simply were to kill the goose and cut it open.* But when the deed was done, not a single golden egg did he find, and his precious goose was dead.[48]

"Andrew," Kevin stated, "you are the Golden Goose. And if you don't

---

[48] https://fablesofaesop.com/the-goose-with-the-golden-eggs.html

take care of yourself, you're not going to be of any help to anyone. You're a master at helping people develop business plans. You've got to start a new business today called *Andrew Inc*. You've gotta take care of the goose!"

That hit home. I realized I wasn't in a swing state in my life or with my sweet wife. I had been spreading myself thin, trying to keep one foot in the husband boat, the dad boat, the coach boat, and every other boat in my world without being all in. I was cheating on those I loved most by not showing up as the best version of myself. I knew what I needed to do.

That night I opened up a blank document and created a one-page business plan for *Andrew Inc*. I have spent every day, week, month, and year working toward and refining that plan, taking care of the Golden Goose, and showing up with more to give in each boat I step into.

I think way too many of us are stepping into the boats of our lives in a frantic scramble, with way too much hand power and not enough head power. We are great at working *IN* our businesses, families, relationships, etc. and pretty terrible at working *ON* them. We show up, do what we're asked to do with very little motivation, wipe our hands after we're done and come back the next day and do it all again.

What's missing in this lackadaisical approach is both intentionality and purpose. No surgeon would ever dare stroll into a surgical room and say, "Well, what do we have here today? Heart's not working, huh? Okay, let's see what we can do. Scalpel." Years and years of preparation, practice and planning precede any incision, including right before the surgery. You definitely want confirmation that this surgeon knows exactly what they're doing before you say, "Nighty night," as the anesthesia lulls you out of consciousness.

And yet all too often, we step into these boats in some kind of trance-like state, pretending to be all in, while in all realty, being totally out of swing.

So, here's a simple strategy to help you develop your own one-page plan to get into swing. You can call it *Amber, Inc*. or whatever your name is if you'd like. The title can certainly come later.

A SWING STATE GPS or 1-3-5

Just as a GPS in your car or on your phone helps you stay on track and arrive at your destination with as few hiccups and off-roading as possible, the 1-3-5 or GPS allows you to focus on what you want most in your life and map out a simple path to get you there.

The "1" or "G" stands for the 1 Goal you are working toward.

The "3" or "P" stands for the 3 Priorities that will ensure your attainment of the 1 Goal.

The "5" or "S" stands for up to 5 Strategies for each Priority that you can put into place to nail the Priorities.

When you're done, you have a one-page plan with up to fifteen strategies that you can focus on to achieve your most important goal, or desired state of being, putting you into a gratifying, rhythmic swing state.

In developing your personal plan to be in swing, consider the following guided exercise to help you build out your 1-3-5 or GPS:

1 (Goal)...What does swing look like for you? What does your *best you* look like? What's the one goal here that you desire?

Ex. "Be in a trusting, powerful, creative, connected and loving state, taking breaks to rest when needed to preserve my natural strengths."

3 (Priorities)...What are the top three priorities you can focus on in your life that will guarantee your attainment of that desired state?

Ex. #1 Priority: Spiritual Well-being
  #2 Priority: Physical Health
  #3 Priority: Happy Relationship

5 (Strategies)...What are five strategies for each priority that you can implement that will help you make that priority exactly that, a priority, a higher importance and greater urgency than anything else.

Ex. #1 Priority: Spiritual Well-being

- *Pray or meditate daily for at least ten minutes.*
- *Read one page or more each night to remind me of my spiritual worth.*
- *Take a break one day a week to recenter my spirit and step away from the world.*

- *Journal my gratitudes before I do anything else to start my day.*
- *Go on one spiritual retreat each year to realign with my personal Mission in Life.*

#2 Priority: Physical Health

- *Sweat at least five days a week for thirty minutes or more.*
- *Sleep a minimum of seven hours each night.*
- *Drink a plant-based smoothie five mornings a week.*
- *Find a hobby that I can do at least once a week that involves outdoor physical recreation.*
- *Make sure I fill and drink my water bottle at least four times each day.*

#3 Priority: Happy Relationship

- *Snuggle my companion for thirty seconds and say, "I love you" before getting out of bed.*
- *Commit to and go on at least one date each week.*
- *Plan and enjoy a quarterly overnighter.*
- *Go on one multi-night vacation each year.*
- *Send a gratitude text randomly throughout the day.*

Now, imagine taking that one-page plan and waking up every morning to see it on the bathroom mirror as you get ready for the day. To keep this new skillset simple and powerful, I highly recommend you review this during your weekly 411 Meeting, making time on your calendar for the upcoming week to implement your intended strategies. This is also a perfect time to read that "1" Goal, what swing looks like for you and evaluate how well you're doing. Remember, what we focus on expands. And where attention goes, energy flows. So, whatever we give energy to, grows.

Think of your 1-3-5 as an organic document, able to evolve in an ever-changing environment called Your Life. This is not something that has to be set in stone, never to adapt or be modified. As you go back to this plan on a consistent basis, you'll notice where small tweaks can be made, adding up to vast improvements over time. You may even change up the order of your priorities or recognize that the "1" Goal itself is not exactly what you truly wanted. And that's the beauty of it; this plan will, like the motion of the ocean, flow *with* you rather than rocking you right out of your boat.

I promise you, and I don't take promises lightly, that if you will invest the energy needed to identify what your swing state looks like for you, prioritize how you can get there and on a daily basis work on the necessary strategies, you will open up a version of yourself that will blow you away (not literally, of course). Seriously though, this is just the tip of the iceberg. When you put this much intentionality into growing yourself, God and the Universe will match your offering with opportunities, relationships and resources that will leave you speechless. Try it, I dare you.

Remember George Yeoman Pocock's words? "The closer a crew can come to that ideal—maintaining a good swing while rowing at a high rate—the closer they are to rowing on another plane, the plane on which champions row."

This plane is waiting for you. Intentionality is the key to unlocking your potential. **Strength of the Oak**.

My 1-3-5

Goal or Desired Swing State:

_____

_____

Priority #1 _____

1 _____

2 _____

3 _____

4 _____

5 _____

Priority #2 _____

    1 _____

    2 _____

    3 _____

    4 _____

    5 _____

Priority #3 _____

    1 _____

    2 _____

    3 _____

    4 _____

    5 _____

CHAPTER TWELVE

The Consecration of Your Humanness

"I don't like human nature, but I do like human beings."
—*Ellen Glasglow*

Let's continue to be honest with one another, life is tricky. But doesn't it seem like some of us make it more challenging than it needs to be? Have you ever stopped for a moment, looked around and asked yourself, "What am I doing? I'm being ridiculous!" I know I have, more often than I'd like to admit.

In these wake-up call kind of moments, it's as if the Universe is shaking up my little bubble for a second, declaring, "Hello! Little human! What do you think you're doing? There's a much greater work going on here and what you're wasting energy on is kind of insignificant."

Oh, yeah. Thank you, Universe! Geez, how did I get so out of whack?

I love it when this happens! Yes, life is hard. But we don't have to overcomplicate it. I think that we unknowingly run this ridiculous pattern to justify *not* hitting our goals *nor* becoming the best we possibly can be. Can we get rid of this sweeping infestation of needless drama, please? We owe it to ourselves and each other.

The world needs us to lead in a state of flow, making the absolute most of our God-given gifts, cultivating all the good around us, and eliminating the excess garbage that seems to be drowning the hopes and dreams of our generation.

We are human. Our nature has been conditioned to fall. Yet our capacity to rise is as simple as flipping a switch here and there. Let's talk about what some of these might look like and how we can make things just a little bit easier on all of us.

STOP TAKING LIFE SO SERIOUSLY: BE INTENTIONALLY UNINTENTIONAL

One of the questions that I ask in a Coaching Prep Form that my clients fill out before each coaching session is this: On a scale of 1-10, how intentional have you been this past week? Sometimes a client will put a number down that's smaller than I would have expected. When I inquire about their response, it goes something like this:

"Well, I was on vacation, so I wasn't intentional at all!"

I will respond with, "Did you intentionally plan that vacation?"

And they answer, "Yeah, of course."

So, I reply, "Then you were totally intentional!"

More often than not, this elicits a lightbulb of sorts that helps them understand something that they and you, may have never considered--intentionally being unintentional is requisite to a big life!

There's an ancient story in Native American history that tells of a family pioneering from one land to another.[49] Wandering through the wilderness, they rely upon hunting and gathering to provide sustenance for their livelihood. At one point, their bows lose their spring and they are unable to hunt for food. The strength of the spring in the bow creates the necessary force to propel an arrow forward with maximum impact. How does a wooden bow lose its spring? It's left tightly strung for too long. A bow must not be high-strung when not in use.

The parallel for our lives is almost too perfect, isn't it? We, like a finely crafted wooden bow, must unwind, releasing all tension, when not in action.

This can happen as we create what I call "white space," time in our schedules to be intentionally unintentional. White space is imperative to our strength and ability to continue growing. This time is the rest between notes in a piece of music that we adore. It's the intense quietude just moments before the sun crests over the

---

[49] The Book of Mormon, 1 Nephi 16:18-22.

morning horizon. It's the break between reps when you're lifting weights. This time is one of renewal, restoration, regeneration, recreation and preservation.

Look at your calendar, right now if you can, and tell me, where do you have white space today, this week, this month, this year? Where have you intentionally blocked time to relax and be completely unintentional?

My guess is that most of us swing to one of two polar opposites on this spectrum--we either have way too much and are not making the most of our precious gift of life or we don't have any and we are worn out and ineffective or getting ready to snap.

An old Chinese proverb says, "Tension is who you think you should be. Relaxation is who you are." Ahhhh....

So, be who you are! Make YOU a priority. Intentionally plan time at least once or twice a day, if not more, for a few moments up to an hour or more if you so desire, to unstring the bow. Meditation, naps, listening to music, watching or listening to something entertaining, taking a bath, reading a book, sitting outside, doing nothing, make relaxation a routine.

What about your week? Same thing. Plan a day, half a day, a few hours each week to do something that is super selfish, for nobody other than yourself. Make sure it fills your bucket and leaves you better, stronger, with more to give.

Expand this to each month, quarter and definitely each year. There should be *at least* one full day a year, if not a week or more, for you to unplug, unwind and be totally unintentional with uninterrupted YOU time. This is as essential to your well-being and vivacity as a good night's sleep. It's playtime and recreation--you're re-creating the best you possible!

Please do it. And start small. Look at today and make sure that your intentionality with your goals is non-negotiable, **Strength of the Oak**. And let's become just as serious about your white space, **Strength of the Willow**. You deserve it!

Journal Entry 🖊 *Where do I commit to making white space in my schedule? What will this do for me that maybe I've never experienced before? Who can best help me with this?*

LAUGH AT YOURSELF

"In my belief, you cannot deal with the most serious things in the world unless you also understand the most amusing."
—Winston Churchill

Have you ever watched a child do something so absurd that you automatically smiled or did everything in your power to hold back a laugh that was bursting inside? It's quite the conundrum. Their behavior is ridiculous and you may actually want to be mad at them, and yet the laughter cannot be suppressed! Sometimes we have to hide our faces so they can't see our amusement.

How is it that we can find such hilarity in a youngster's nonsensical performance, when on the flip side, we cast such extreme criticisms and punishments toward ourselves? That's pretty unfair, if you ask me.

When it comes to children, we know that it's age-appropriate behavior and they'll grow out of it. And if it's someone else's kid, we're often even more forgiving. But when it comes to ourselves, we seem to lack that long-term perspective. We're not so much an observer as we are a participant. Rather than knowing that there's another scene coming and the whole production will soon be over, we get stuck in the moment and paint a self-portrait as if this snapshot will define our legacy and character for the rest of our lives! If that were true, then we certainly wouldn't be laughing. What a hurtful belief!

One of my daughters, Avery, was blessed with this gift of laughter from infancy. As a baby, the more tired she got, the more she'd laugh. We have awesome memories of bedtime routines when her older sister Kella, a toddler at the time, would also be rolling in laughter from watching her baby sister bring so much joy to our family. Avery has continued to be a beacon of light by diffusing overly serious situations by helping all around her find what's funny in otherwise frustrating and tense times. She's a breath of fresh air and a great example to so many.

Let's take a step back and do for ourselves what we do so easily for children and like children, *laugh!* Allow the comedic nature of most things to roll to you and through you with a grin and chuckle. Your face will shine brighter, your abs will be stronger and your heart will be lighter. Your body deserves a break! And your spirit will appreciate one too!

In his groundbreaking book, *Your Erroneous Zones,* Wayne Dyer taught:

> *"Perhaps the single most outstanding characteristic of healthy people is their unhostile sense of humor… Why waste your present being angry when laughing feels so good… decide whether to carry around anger or to develop a sense of humor that will give you and others one of the most priceless gifts of all–laughter."*

Journal Entry 🖊 *What would a bit of humor, laughter and lightheart-edness do for my spirit?*

MAKE MORE MISTAKES

> *"Every adversity, every failure, every heartache carries with it the seed of an equal or greater benefit."*
> —Napoleon Hill

Fast forward about seven or eight years from toddlerhood to fifth grade for my oldest daughter, Kella. I had one main objective for her last year of elementary school, "Fail at something." Yup. She looked at me like I was crazy, too, but I even told her teacher, Mr. Z., "If Kella's not failing, she's not learning." And so, I'd ask her frequently, "What did you fail at today?" She pridefully responded, week in and week out, "Nothing Dad!"

At the end of the school year, she reminded me that she had beaten me at my own game. She had succeeded in never failing. "Oh, really?" I asked with a tinge of doubt in my voice. "Didn't you run for Class President three times without being elected?" She quipped back, "That doesn't count! That's not school." We had a meaningful conversation about education, school and what real learning is all about.

I can almost guarantee that Kella will not remember hardly any of the curriculum she aced in the fifth grade, but she will always remember the determined grit she picked up as she kept on running for Class President. I was so proud of her! That's a life lesson with a long shelf life.

After that school year, we made it a point to not simply ask around the dinner table, "What was the best part of your day?" We also decided to include, "What mistakes did you make today? What did you learn?" We even made a list that we kept in the kitchen to record our mistakes and share them openly, just as we would our successes, because they're equally as important to our growth, and definitely worth celebrating.

What about you? How can you bring greater awareness to your mistakes, the tuition required for a "Master of Life" degree?

What if you journaled just one thing each day that you learned from. That kind of awareness would become your SUPERPOWER! I'm not kidding. One of my greatest mentors taught me that change is 90% awareness. And with that kind of a habit, you'd be changing and growing so much that people would hardly recognize you!

I say lean in with all you've got to the bending of the willow. You're not going to break when you embrace your shortcomings. Again, where attention goes, energy flows. And where energy flows, strength increases. Our weaknesses really can become strengths. But you can't ignore them. That's when things snap. Welcome the flaws; they're not fatal. Fortitude is waiting in the background of each and every ounce of deficiency.

"Failures, repeated failures," said C.S. Lewis, "are finger posts on the road to achievement. One fails forward toward success."[50]

---

[50] Readers Digest, "Education Begins at Home", February 1944.

Journal Entry 🖋 *What will I add to my daily and/or weekly routine to celebrate the successes of my failing forward?*

THE FLOW OF SELF-RELIANCE INTO INTERDEPENDENCE

I invite you to consider a fundamental formula for a greater and more harmonious life with yourself and all around you:

Formula for Self-Reliance

An indomitable commitment to
our Life Mission, values and principles
+
Intentionality to create
the absolute best for our lives
+
The ability to move forward
making mistakes, laughing and being unintentional when appropriate
=
Grounded in a modern-day state that seems
to be losing numbers (self-reliance).

Self-reliance is a foundational, **Strength of the Oak** characteristic of those who rise to the greatest potential within them. It is this independence that boldly states, "I know who I am. I know what I must do. I will move forward regardless of others' support. I am more than enough. Join me if you so desire and if not, please step aside. If you change your mind, let me know. I'll see you later!"

I'm not the first to mention this proverb:

If you want to go fast, go alone. If you want to go far, go together.

What then, is that vital relationship between independence and interdependence?

Milton Mayeroff offered this timeless perspective, "In the sense in which a man can ever be said to be at home in the world, he is at home not through dominating or explaining or appreciating, but through caring and being cared for...Through caring and being cared for man experiences himself as part of nature."[51]

Yes, we must be self-reliant, able to act independent of others to find our own necessary roots. And then, we, like the wonders of nature, can have something both to give and receive to fulfill all that we possibly can. It is a **Strength of the Willow** wisdom that accepts with abundant gratitude all that the world has to offer. Humility and meekness recognize how much more we can become when we allow others to care for us while we continue to care for ourselves and others.

I learned this harrowing lesson in a way I would have never anticipated. I call it "leveling up."

LEVELING UP

Man, was I *sick!* And not your run-of-the-mill, cold or flu kind of sick.

No, day in and day out I was drained of every ounce of energy, hardly able to even get up off the couch or out of bed. I'd never experienced anything like it. Every square inch of my body ached, from the hair on the top of my head to the deepest marrow in my bones. My head pounded, just like it would after attending a live rock concert, only there was no entertainment, and no letup. I tried to find distraction in reading or watching something... anything! There was no relief whatsoever. I was in the middle of writing this book and I didn't even attempt to touch the manuscript, not once. The thought alone just made my head hurt even worse.

The fevers and the chills felt like they'd never go away–hot...cold... hot...cold...hot...cold. My whining and complaining were constant. It was self-pity and anger, all intertwined into a terribly deplorable attitude. My poor family! I was even getting tired of being around me. If

---

[51] On Caring, Milton Mayeroff, PERENNIAL LIBRARY, 1971, pp. 2, 87

you were to ask sweet Chari, "Who had it worse, you or him?" She'd smile and lie that it was definitely me.

Sleeping was hell, for both of us. I knew the rejuvenating rest was essential for my recovery, though trying to get it was seemingly impossible. I'd often go to the couch in the bonus room or the bed in our guest room, hoping for some reprieve.

I woke up in the middle of one of these miserable nights, around 12:30 a.m. or 1:00 a.m., having tossed and turned for what felt like forever. I was restless, in and out of a feverish delirium, aching and moaning and groaning, knowing I wasn't actually going to die but feeling like I definitely wanted to. It had been twelve days of this tormenting illness and thinking it had been long enough, I offered a simple and humble prayer, "Heavenly Father, is there anything else you want me to learn before I can be healed and whole again?"

The answer came as clear and concise as anytime in my life, "You are going through this to better develop a love for *all* people. This is molding you to be more compassionate."

As I laid there, my mind wandered back to the sacred words of the blessing I had received when I was fourteen. This was the same time that I'd first understood my Life Mission. Those guiding and comforting words had been typed in a beautiful letter so that I could easily access them, which I did often. Through the years I had read and re-read that blessing at least a hundred times. One of the admonitions that repeatedly stuck out was my call to develop a love for *all* people.

A million thoughts and feelings raced through my mind and heart as I realized I had never been able to truly empathize with those suffering through physical pain and illness. I had never experienced this kind of soul-stretching tribulation to any great extent in my life, up until that moment. I began to recognize that without my own experiential knowledge of this degree of pain, I lacked the ability to connect with and love my brothers and sisters from a deep place of care and concern.

All of this knowledge poured into me in what seemed like an instant. And then the words, "Your suffering now has meaning and you don't need to suffer any more," rushed into my mind. The tears and emotions

STRENGTH OF THE OAK

streamed from a place in my heart I didn't know existed. It was a relief unlike any I'd ever felt. It was gratitude, exhaustion, love, strength, mercy, grace and so much more all wrapped into one.

As I pondered the spiritual learnings of this answered prayer, I remembered Viktor Frankl's teachings from *Man's Search For Meaning*, "In some way, suffering ceases to be suffering at the moment it finds a meaning, such as the meaning of a sacrifice." I knew that I no longer had to suffer as these twelve days of misery now had powerful meaning for me. This experience cast a new light onto those I had loved before but had no clue what they were really going through.

Melissa was a dear client of mine who frequently fought through debilitating migraines. My older sister, Aleesa, has endured the same challenge as well for nearly all of her life.

A close friend, Blair, dealt with neuropathy, causing weakness, numbness and unbearable pain in his feet–way too much for his frail, eighty-two-year-old body.

One of my neighbors, Jeremy, was assisted in his morning routine by a professional caregiver and put to bed nightly by his selfless wife. Jeremy was a quadriplegic who never uttered a single word regarding his unimaginable discomfort.

I'm not pretending my week and a half of personal agony gave me 100% understanding and empathy for all who experience physical pain. There's no way I could say, "Hey, listen. I've been there, done that. I understand what it's like for you." That's unfair and honestly, demeaning. What I can say now, with a bit more weight and much more sincerity is, "I'm sorry. I've had my own unique physical trials and I can't imagine what this must be like for you. How can I help?"

Reinvigorated with my new revelation, I was almost certain I'd wake up and be done with all of this, that I'd finally be on the ups, ready to get back to living. My suffering had been transformed–transformed into sacrifice.

Now I love that word, "sacrifice." When we break down the Latin roots we find *sacer*, which means "sacred" or "holy" and *facere*, which means "to make" or "to do." When our suffering takes on meaning and turns into sacrifice, we are transformed, made into something sacred and holy.

I now see this personal experience as necessary to my spiritual growth. Compassion was the next level for my love of mankind. And in order to get there, suffering, meaning and sacrifice were the essential equation.

With this sprouting compassion I've also been surprised to find that I've become less afraid of pain and suffering. I understand the meaning behind it and get to choose that meaning when faced with the opportunity. The physical pain of those around me, along with all other forms of psychological and spiritual distress that we see plaguing our agonized world, has morphed from something that I truly was afraid of into an invitation I openly embrace. I'm grateful for this divine gift of compassion that came when I needed it most.

Journal Entry 🖊 *Where can you see opportunities in your current life situation that are beckoning you to become even more compassionate? How can your acceptance of these experiences allow for greater love and less resistance? What else could this kind of an approach open up for you?*

CHAPTER THIRTEEN

Attributes of the Divine

"Character is like a tree and reputation like a shadow. The shadow is what we think of it; the tree is the real thing."
—Abraham Lincoln

"It isn't fair!" says every child, sometime or another in their life. I used to say it. You used to say it. Our kids now do it too.

Where does this come from? Why do we fight for fairness? Come on, do we really want every decision we make, every item we own, every relationship we hold dear, to be judged and found to be of *equal* value? Is that justice? Is it that we want everyone to be treated the exact same and always have good rewarded for good and bad for bad? There's got to be more to it than that, right?

As a parent, it's excruciating to sit back and watch, wincing in pain, while our children suffer the inevitable consequences of their choices. In our house, my wife and I have decided we really don't want to have to experience this on a large scale, with criminal charges and prison sentences as our kids grow into adolescents and adults. So, Chari created what we call our Agreement Book. If something's not working in our home, we come together in a Family Meeting and discuss what the new, mutually respectful agreement will be and what happens if it's not upheld. We then write up a contract with signatures and all. Everyone signs, as all ages are honored (and learning can never happen too young).

When conflicts arise, we often say, "Hey, didn't we already talk about this? What does the Agreement Book say?" We then ask the kids to read us what we previously agreed to and then let the consequences follow. As grueling as it can be to listen to the moaning and groaning, including the complaints of just how "unfair" the family system is, our children are learning to reap what they sow...and to therefore sow *carefully*. We're hoping that justice will be a lot easier to learn with a vacuum and dust rag in hand rather than handcuffs in the backseat of a police car.

STRENGTH OF THE WILLOW: *Mercy Unmatched*

> *"For the Lord thy God is a merciful God; he will not*
> *forsake thee, neither destroy thee, nor forget"*
> *—Deuteronomy 4:31*

Mercy, the twin sister of justice, is compassion in action. This gentle treatment of another might seem undeserved to onlookers. And that's precisely the point. Mercy looks beyond behavior or qualifications deserving of kindness.

When God needed a new king in Israel, he reminded the prophet Samuel, "the Lord seeth not as man seeth; for man looketh on the outward appearance, but the Lord looketh on the heart" (1 Samuel 16:7). David, the youngest of Jesse's eight sons, farmer and sheep breeder, and seemingly unfit for royalty, was chosen. Good choice! It was he who ended up slaying Goliath.

To look on someone's heart means we recognize that everyone is doing the best they can with the resources they've been given. Mercy respects other people's models of the world.

When a baby is learning about gravity and depth perception and repeatedly throws their food onto the ground, we don't give up on Day One. Mercy acknowledges age-appropriate behavior and patiently allows for development. And in the grand scheme of things, aren't we all children in our spiritual quest to become like our Heavenly Parents? Jesus loved little children, and treated all, regardless of their age, with a care and compassion that calls for emulation.

But, mercy, as significant as it is, cannot and will not *ever* rob justice. Christ was an advocate for those that were less advantaged in society. He took a stand and opened his mouth in clear condemnation toward all who sought to harm the weak, the weary, his "little ones."[52]

STRENGTH OF THE OAK: *Speaking Up*

Audrey is a beautiful example of someone who, with the help of family, friends and professionals, stood up for herself and won an internal war that had been waged for far too long. I was fortunate enough to be on the front lines of battle when victory seemed despairingly out of reach.

From the outside looking in, everyone thought Audrey was happy. She had more than mastered the art of pretending. Burning the candle at both ends, this thirty-seven-year-old woman balanced a blended family with seven kids while being the breadwinner with a full-time job. After trying to manage this precarious dance for over four years, Audrey was desperate for a change. The pressure piled up as she tried in desperation to keep it together "for the sake of my kids."

What she wasn't telling anyone, however, was that she didn't want to live anymore. There was a dark, tyrannical secret that no one could ever know…

Having been sexually abused as a young girl and never learning to love herself, Audrey was a prime target for further harm as an adult. Originally believing that the sacred union of marriage would be a safe place, she was abruptly and horridly shocked. Her police officer husband, Tom, lived a public life of protecting and serving the community. His private life was far from that.

Audrey agreed to things that she knew were wrong in order to keep him happy. "I was a puppet and couldn't break away from the strings. His needs were stealing pieces of my soul," she later shared with me while in tears. She had learned to disassociate from her body, not wanting to exist in that space of sexual abuse any longer. This spilled into all aspects of her life until one night, she simply couldn't take it anymore.

---

[52] see Matthew 18:6

Her thoughts of suicide turned into a premeditated plan with which she was determined to follow through. Audrey entered her boys' rooms first and kissed them goodnight, knowing this would be her last time tucking them in. Slowly walking into her daughter's room, she looked into those big, brown eyes and discovered something she hadn't expected. *If I go through with this, she will follow in my footsteps.* That little girl, her little girl, saved her life. She knew something had to change and it needed to happen fast.

The next day, Audrey told Tom that she'd decided to move forward in hiring me as her coach. He'd previously shot down the idea, not wanting to let anyone in that could possibly loosen the tight, controlling grip he had on his wife. She posed it this time as an opportunity to build her business and make more money for the family. When he heard the idea of more money, Tom was in.

And Audrey's business did grow. She began to let some of her walls down, just enough for me to peek over and see that things were not okay. I had no idea what was really going on behind the scenes, the abuse. She kept pretending. So, I brought in some backup, my business partner and sister, who is a highly skilled and sought-after marriage coach. Working hand in hand, we believed that their relationship could be salvaged with the right help.

After a couple of months of working together, things only got worse. My sister and I just couldn't seem to put our finger on all of it. What was really going on behind closed doors, and how could we help?

I knew one thing for sure—I did not want to sit by feeling so small and powerless to do anything. I was compelled to do something to uphold the virtue of women who were not being treated like a queen. Ultimately, however, it was all up to Audrey. I could only empower her to make greater, nobler choices. And then, one night, she did.

Tom was yelling at Audrey's son, calling him terrible names. As she watched her little boy's face melt with tears at the kitchen table, she realized that she didn't have to stay. At that moment, Tom told her to get in the car so they could talk without the kids being around.

In an uncontrollable rage, he accelerated over 100 MPH and

threatened to flip the car. He screamed out, "You disrespected me in front of your son by not choosing my side!" As he thrust his fist upward and furiously punched the ceiling of the car, Audrey trembled. *Next time, that fist will probably be coming for me.*

Sitting in fear, her survival instincts kicked in and she knew she needed to calm him down. She praised him and told him how sorry she was, playing the game of letting the abuser win so they could have some peace. . .and stay alive. As his anger slowed, so did the car.

The next day, Audrey made an emergency call to me and my sister and described everything that was taking place—the cruelty of constant name-calling, the endless fights, her daughter's self-harm, a young son full of anger from being physically hurt by Tom, an older son pulling the three kids together in his room and holding them close when Mom was in trouble and the sickening years of sexual grooming and manipulation that shattered Audrey's world.

Calling on her "team of angels," her loving parents, four close friends and two coaches in her corner, we got her checked into a hotel room under a different name and the journey to save her life and her kids' was underway. There was nothing easy about this undertaking, but as Audrey leaned on her team, she learned to pick herself up and heal from deep wounds. She chose self-love and compassion and gave herself the most marvelous gift she'd ever received.

This newfound bravery enabled her to recreate a life that she and her kids always knew they deserved. They now live in a home that is full of light where love abounds. Her children are thriving. Happiness and peace run through them.

One year later, Audrey told me something I will never forget. She said, "I wake up grateful, every day, that I didn't follow through with my plan to end the pain, that I chose a life worth having. My goal now is to show people they do not have to go through that pain. Emotional and sexual abuse are not normal and you can escape it. If I can share anything, it is that you are worth fighting for and this life is beautiful. I can honestly say that I am truly happy and no longer need to pretend to be."

From our corner, we couldn't be prouder as we celebrate Audrey's freedom and commitment to help other women find *their* voice. She is building a coaching movement to save lives, to protect and serve in a most dignified way. She is a warrior of light, a bright beacon of hope for all. Her story is a key witness to the fact that each of us can find unbeatable and unbreakable strength when we speak up, loud and clear…together. **Strength of the Oak.**

Journal Entry ✐ *Is there a person or situation that is bringing worry, angst, or unease to your world at the moment? How might your silence or speaking up affect the outcome of that challenge? Maybe there's been one in the past. How could this type of proactive response have changed things? Maybe there's one coming up in the near future. Do you need to be heard or can silence be your sword?*

STRENGTH OF THE WILLOW: *Frankly Forgive*

> *"The weak can never forgive. Forgiveness*
> *is the attribute of the strong."*
> —Mahatma Gandhi

Consider this: When someone wrongs you, what other options do you have, besides forgiveness? Anger, resentment, jealousy, revenge? Honestly, whoever said, "I wish I had held on to those negative emotions and consuming thoughts longer and not been so quick to forgive and let it all go?"

What are you refusing to forgive? What are you missing out on? While all this continues to fester, are you actually growing in your life, personally and professionally? What impact is this having on your relationships with those that mean the most to you? What's the price you pay in other aspects of your life when you viciously or justifiably hang on to your pride?

When we choose not to forgive, we are losing so slowly that we think we are winning. It's sad. Death by a thousand cuts.

Jesus, the greatest victor to ever step into our earthly arena, imparted words of wisdom for all regarding the blessings that accompany forgiveness.

- "For if ye forgive men their trespasses, your heavenly Father will also forgive you" (Matthew 6:14).
- "Forgive, and ye shall be forgiven" (Luke 6:37).
- "And forgive us our debts, as we forgive our debtors" (Matthew 6:12).

No one is about to dismiss the immensity of his oral teachings, although it was his actions, up to the very end of his life, that made his words so powerful and unforgettable.

Of his final seven recorded statements while hanging on the cross, the one that surely caused the greatest bewilderment to the people there along with the many scholars, students and curious disciples since that time, "Father, forgive them; for they know not what they do" (Luke 23:34). At that moment of intense pain and suffering, enough for his heart to literally burst, there he was, letting go of the hatred that had been hurled upon him by those Roman soldiers.

How? How did he do it? I think I can begin to understand why. But, how?

It's often said that you've got to be able to walk a mile in someone else's shoes to understand them, right? Jesus didn't just walk a mile, he ran, crawled, listened, felt, cried, rejoiced and bled *ALL* the miles in *ALL* of our shoes, not just once, but twice, in both the Garden of Gethsemane and on the Cross of Calvary. It was this unmatched empathy and incomprehensible understanding that pulled at him as he pleaded for his persecutors' forgiveness, having already paid the painful price of their horrific sins being acted out even as he spoke.

So, "How?" we ask. The answer is simple, and not the least bit easy. Bruce R. McConkie, a powerful scholar on the life of Christ, explained that in this moment, Jesus recognized that these soldiers had no choice but to do the will of Pilate and those whose minions they were. Christ was not asking the Father to forgive the soldiers and his accusers of their sins. He was simply asking that the "deed of crucifixion be not laid at their door; let the responsibility rest with the Jews and with the Procurator of Rome, not with these who were doing—albeit in a gross and cruel manner—no more than they had been commanded to do."[53]

Jesus saw what no one else would--that these men were probably doing the absolute best they could with the hand they'd been dealt. Hence, the Son asked the Father to forgive his crucifiers, knowing that his atoning blood would completely cover the demands of justice laid upon them, should they choose, at a later time, to repent of this atrocity.

When we allow others' actions and our suffering to canker within us, long after the misdeed, we are giving our attention to the wrongdoing. And remember, where attention goes, energy flows. And where energy flows, things grow. Our unwillingness to forgive strengthens the effect of the transgression. And while the offender may have made amends with their Creator, the sin now sits with us. We are now suffering not because of that person, we are suffering 100% from our own self-inflicted wounds, harboring hate and holding back forgiveness.

The former president of South Africa and Nobel Peace Prize recipient, Nelson Mandela, spent twenty-seven years in prison for his resistance to the Apartheid. The Apartheid was a national system of institutionalized racial oppression that started in 1948. It denied non-white South Africans basic rights, like the right to vote or even the right to swim at the beach.[54]

Mandela's impassioned fight for human equality and a democratic government landed him in Robben Island, a maximum-security prison, sentenced to years of hard labor. During this time, he was confined to a small cell, where the floor was his bed and a bucket was his toilet. Mandela was only allowed one visitor each year for thirty minutes, and he could write and receive just one letter every six months.[55]

---

[53] Bruce R. McConkie, The Mortal Messiah: From Bethlehem to Calvary (Salt Lake City: Deseret Book, 1981), 4:211–12.

[54] https://en.wikipedia.org/wiki/Apartheid

[55] https://www.pbs.org/wgbh/pages/frontline/shows/mandela/prison/

After being released early (twenty-seven years instead of a lifetime sentence of imprisonment), Mandela would later share the following in his autobiography, *Long Walk to Freedom*, "As I walked out the door toward the gate that would lead to my freedom, I knew if I didn't leave my bitterness and hatred behind, I'd still be in prison." It was Mandela's remarkable vision for his own life—and the possibilities that awaited millions of oppressed fellow brothers and sisters of his beloved nation—that empowered him to move forward with forgiveness.

Like Nelson Mandela, Viktor Frankl and so many other exceptional examples, we too can commit to lovingly letting go of our hurt and bitterness (as well as any we may be causing others) by offering the divine gift of forgiveness. Let us make a decision, right here and right now, that we will always choose to forgive. Once that decision, that commitment has been declared, the line has been drawn in the sand. This means we will no longer go through the painstaking process of putting unnecessary energy, heavy negativity or strenuous thought into our response to another's offenses. The decision has already been made.

THE STING OF NOT FORGIVING

Have you ever been bothered by a swarm of hornets or wasps? There they are, diving down and defending their territory, doing their duty from a place of survival. And there you are, swatting and cursing, trying to protect yourself from becoming the victim of a vicious sting. You're probably going to vacate the premises, ASAP.

To me, this is a lot like how most of us approach the process of forgiveness. We try to swat others away. We curse their existence. And then we leave, speaking of their wretched place in our lives. This could go on forever, day after day, year after year. They're not going to just go away. We hold on, for far too long, to nasty nests that house these disturbing guests. Wouldn't it be better to just remove the nest, to simply forgive and free ourselves from further annoyance and pain?

"But how?" you'll undoubtedly ask. "I've been stung so many times and the buzzing haunts me in my dreams."

Do you have a bee-sting story that bears repeating? Here's mine:

Imagine me, twenty-one years old, visiting my older sister, Aleesa, and her three little kids, and facing a fearsome wasp nest. I was ready to show up as a hero of an uncle, conquering the assailants who threatened any and all who approached the front porch. I asked for appropriate attire and weaponry, a hooded coat, ski goggles, oven mitts, a broomstick and a tennis racket were provided. I really wish we'd snapped a photo before I began my epic assault!

To my amazement, and that of the juvenile audience who was rolling in laughter at my preferred pest control methods, I somehow managed to get stung while taking down the enemy's mother ship and disposing of it. I didn't know I was allergic. If I did, I would have smartened up and added some snow pants and maybe larger oven mitts or *something* to better protect myself.

An allergic reaction set it in fast, and my sister gave me some Benadryl to nullify the growing welts. After nursing my wounds and dressing the nieces and nephews in my infamous battle suit, I decided it was time to end the raid and head home.

I guess I'd never taken an antihistamine before. As I drove home, I remember thinking, *Man, that sun sure is bright! I can hardly keep my eyes open. Why does it have to be shining right in my face?* My eyelids were crashing down like a garage door off its track. I had to force them to stay open for the five-minute drive.

When I got home, I slept from three in the afternoon clear through the night and into the next morning. I guess I got a double dose of Benadryl, by accident, from my well-meaning sister. When all was said and done, Aleesa's kids and any unwary neighbors were now safe. I had a newly discovered allergy. And we all cherish a great family story that gets told time and time again.

While I personally don't have a lifetime sentence prison experience like Nelson Mandela, I do have another story of getting stung, one that hurt a bit more than that of my early adulthood adventures: The Divorce.

At first, I was my own worst enemy. I really did take *all* of the blame for our marriage failing. I beat myself up, ruthlessly. I believed that I was single-handedly responsible to my God and our three girls for our family's falling apart. It took years of therapy, counseling with loving family and loyal friends, rebuilding my shattered self-esteem and some honest pleading and praying for self-forgiveness in order for me to feel the weight lifted. It was an arduous journey of inner work to accept the fact that we each, my first wife and I, owned 100% of our own baggage that led to the divorce.

Here's where the miracle happened. As soon as I'd found the grace necessary to forgive myself, I was free to forgive her as well. As I look back on that challenging process, my individual learnings, along with those of the hundreds I've coached to their own places of accountability, acceptance and spiritual liberty, all of these have formed what I now call *7 Proven Steps to Forgiveness of Others and Yourself.*

When appropriately applied, these transformative steps have produced miraculous results of healing. Some of the individuals I've been fortunate enough to work with might have previously been labeled "irreparably damaged." No soul, in my opinion, should ever have to be doomed to shameful victimhood. There is hope for all of us.

This is how we do it:

7 PROVEN STEPS TO FORGIVENESS OF OTHERS AND YOURSELF

1. **Acknowledge and Assess:** Acknowledge the pain and assess the damage. What have you felt that hurts so badly? Name those emotions. What did you believe to be true about yourself because of this? What did you make this offense mean about you?
2. **See the Light:** What do you gain from holding on to all of this? Could you get this or something even better when you let go of the problem? What would you rather experience instead? What would life look like without this? What's the light at the other end of this dark tunnel?
3. **Get Permission:** Ask yourself for permission to be free. Are you open to the possibility of a better way? Allow yourself to say *'yes.'*

4. **Preserve the Learnings:** What do you need to learn from this experience, the learning of which will allow you to let go of the pain (the negative emotions or limiting beliefs)? Write this down. Preserve the positive learnings.

5. **Step into the Light:** How will this lightened load benefit you moving forward? What's possible now?

6. **Seal the Deal:** What actions do you need to take to really seal the deal and be 100% free to move forward? Do you want to approach the person or will a simple letter that can later be burned or deleted do the trick?

7. **Ensure Protection:** If you need to protect yourself from potential heartache in the future, set up safeguards by asking others to help. Decide what your boundaries are that you'll never cross again. Make a plan for protection.

What I've laid out for you here is deep work. No joke. A one time reading and a few passing thoughts will not provide the healing necessary for your freedom. You're going to have to mark this page and schedule some time, either right here and now or in the future, to really process these questions and let them sink in. It will be more than worth it. Please, let this one be a tool you try on with serious intent.

I personally have gone through this process numerous times and professionally with hundreds of individuals. It is a proven and powerful way to move beyond the past pain, be fully present to the enriching moments of right now and prevent unneeded hurt in the future. Once we've practiced and polished these seven steps, we can create an unconscious response of always forgiving, no questions asked, like Jesus did.

After a lifetime of forgiving others, seven times seventy, at least, Christ was prepared to spiritually forgive his murderers in the Garden of Gethsemane, and therefore, he knew exactly what to do and say when that moment presented itself on the cross. He was free from their oppression. To me, the miracle is that he offered his persecutors the exact same freedom. That reward of paradise, "a get-out-of-jail-free card," is ours to claim as well, the moment we decide to redeem it.

Choose forgiveness. **Strength of the Willow**.

THE FLIP SIDE OF FORGIVENESS

What about when we've messed up? We opened our big mouths and said something we shouldn't have said. Somehow, we ended up doing the unthinkable, causing harm to another person who didn't deserve it (or maybe they did, but we still know that we were in the wrong). Our words and actions follow us like a dark and looming shadow of shame, a clanking ball and chain of guilt that we just can't seem to shake free. That haunting lingers. We're slowly, painfully, being eaten alive.

There is help here too. Hope resides.

Here's my own, condensed version of the Twelve Steps, from the healing world of A.A., adapted to the process of seeking forgiveness from others. It is honest, simple, solid and true.

7 SOLID STEPS FOR ASKING OTHERS FOR FORGIVENESS

1. **Admit:** Admit to yourself that a joyful life cannot unfold without taking care of this offense.
2. **Believe:** Believe that a Power beyond yourself can bring a restored peace.
3. **Decide:** Make a decision to turn this situation over to the care of God, your Source.
4. **Admit & Ask:** Admit to God the exact nature of your wrongs and ask for his help.
5. **Make Amends:** List out all persons who have been harmed because of the offense and, wherever possible, ask each person for forgiveness.
6. **Repair:** Do all that you can to right the wrong.
7. **Prevent:** Put parameters in place to protect yourself and

others from having to deal with this similar situation in the future. Remember, it's better to prepare and prevent than to repair and repent.

If we're planning on remaining human for the rest of our lives (I know I am) then we're going to need to bookmark these last few pages. Coming back to forgiveness of ourselves and others while seeking forgiveness *from* others is the secret ingredient to a life worth living. It creates room for improvement, space for exploration, a clean slate to learn from and a safety net for every time we fall forward as we make our way home to heaven…and perhaps in bringing heaven here.

CHAPTER FOURTEEN

Love Unfeigned

*"There is nothing I would not do for those who
are really my friends. I have no notion of loving
people by halves; it is not my nature."*
—*Jane Austen*

When we leave this earth, what will we take with us? Will our fame, fortune, investments, collectibles and other prized possessions be of any worth in the hereafter? If not, then what will?

When approached by an eager follower, ready to devote his life to Christianity, "Jesus said unto him, Foxes have holes, and birds of the air have nests; but the Son of man hath not where to lay his head" (Luke 9:58).

Born in a lowly stable, in a town far from his mother and father's home, Jesus never appeared to have much of anything, in terms of material goods. As the King of the Jews--and the whole world which he had created--his kingdom was truly not of this world. There would be no palace, no servants, no succulent meals. His greatest treasures would be his followers, those to whom he could offer a life far greater than any king that could previously or ever provide.

We see that Peter, Jesus' chief apostle, had clearly learned this lesson when he reached out his hand to the lame man and said, "Silver and gold have I none; but such as I have give I thee: In the name of Jesus Christ of Nazareth rise up and walk" (Acts 3:6).

What did Peter offer that Christ taught him through three years of masterful mentoring? I would say *hope*. I would say *love*. Peter offered what he had been given by Jesus since day one--*purpose*.

When we instill hope, love and purpose into another person, we create a bond that lasts through this life and into the next. Those relationships, along with our knowledge and wisdom, is just about all that will really matter when we leave this earthly home.

STRENGTH OF THE OAK: *Love Unfeigned*

> *"Never let a problem to be solved become more important than a person to be loved."*
> —*Thomas S. Monson*

One afternoon, I was walking into my office when someone enthusiastically called out, "Hey, Andrew!" I turned around and a past client of mine had brought his car to a halt and jumped out with a smile as wide as Texas. "We had a baby girl just two weeks ago!"

We embraced and I congratulated him. He reminded me that a few years before they had lost twins due to a miscarriage. Since that time, I had totally forgotten about this experience, as we had fallen out of touch. He became rather emotional and holding back tears said, "You have no idea how much you helped me at that time. Thank you so much, brother! Seriously, I can't even tell you the impact you had on me during all of that." We hugged again and I expressed my gratitude for him and for making an effort to stop and share this beautiful news and special moment with me.

As he pulled away and I walked into my office I thought, *Man! I can't believe that I had completely forgotten about all of those wonderful things happening between us and in his life.* A flood of feelings rushed over me, mostly gratitude, love and humility.

Sometimes we get so caught up in the present moment, that we simply can't remember all of the good from the past. I was profoundly affected by this experience and thanked my Heavenly Father for giving me a glimpse of his work that I was fortunate enough to share a small part in.

Jesus was second to none when it came to nurturing relationships with those around him. Consider a few of these:

Mary and Martha

One day, these two devout sisters received Jesus into their home for what appeared to be a casual, friendly visit. Martha, to whom the dwelling belonged, was "cumbered about much serving" while Mary "sat at Jesus' feet, and heard his word."

Maybe she felt a bit jealous, or unappreciated, or who knows exactly what, but Martha asked, in my own interpretation, "Excuse me, Jesus, don't you see that Mary has left all of this work for me to do alone? Would you mind asking her to help me?"

And then Jesus answered, with soft spoken and tender-hearted words that I dare not alter, "Martha, Martha, thou art careful and troubled about many things: But one thing is needful: and Mary hath chosen that good part, which shall not be taken away from her" (Luke 10:38-42).

Serving the Messiah is a magnificent undertaking. Spending time with him, face to face, conversing in an intimate setting--priceless! It is in moments like these that we are best reminded that when it comes to relationships we value most, love is best spelled *T-I-M-E*.

Jesus knew that his time was short. He was not ungrateful for the service Martha rendered. He most certainly asks us to serve him through our loving acts of kindness to others. He said it himself that, "Inasmuch as ye have done it unto one of the least of these my brethren, ye have done it unto me" (Matthew 25:40). And yet, what he had to offer Mary and Martha in that moment was far greater than any service they might render to him.

He taught them that being a good and grateful receiver of his grace, his time, his attention, his love, was equally important to, if not more so, than giving it back to him.

Their relationship and precious time outweighed any household duties that pressed on anxious Martha's mind.

I see one additional powerful principle of friendship in this encounter. You may have heard something like this at some point in your life: "A real friend is someone who can accept me just the way I am." I like this, sort of. But I like this even better; yes, God does indeed love us exactly as we are right here and right now, but he loves us so much that he absolutely won't leave us like this. Opportunities for complete change, massive growth and infinite spiritual maturity are what he brings to our friendship with him.

Jesus loved Martha way too much to simply let her continue on her path of distracted discipleship. He cared more about her spiritual growth than he did her emotional comfort. I'm sure there had been other friends or family members who had seen this character flaw in her and maybe had held back constructive criticism because of seemingly selfish desires to not look bad or make Martha feel lesser than. Who wants to be that person? Jesus, the truest friend, sacrifices all things selfish as he seeks to help us see what we're actually made of. That's friendship at its finest!

Journal Entry ✎ *What lessons can you learn from Mary and Martha? Do your friends invite you to grow by providing constructive feedback? If not, why? Do you provide your friends with constructive feedback? If not, why? What would need to change in order for you to have those kinds of friendships? What would you observe if this were the case?*

STRENGTH OF THE WILLOW: *Trusting Heavenly Timetables*

Some say that willow trees are short lived. Thirty to eighty years doesn't seem like much compared to hundreds and even thousands of years that some oaks have been estimated to live. Although the willow tree might not live as long as others, it has an incredible capacity to produce new life, differently than does the oak. A willow branch can be cut and simply placed in the ground in the Spring and a new tree will soon take root.

Though Jesus' life on this earth may have appeared, to some of his followers at the time, to have been cut way too short, only thirty-three years, he chose to be planted in a new location, his heavenly home.

Having broken the bands of death that first Easter morning, his resurrection offers life to all.

I lay down my life, that I might take it again.
No man taketh it from me, but I lay it down of myself. I have
power to lay it down, and I have power to take it again…
And I give unto them eternal life; and they shall never
perish, neither shall any man pluck them out of my hand.
—John 10:17,18,28

Why do we question God's timing? No other creation of his actually keeps track of time. A doe doesn't count how many weeks until delivery. Bears aren't using alarm clocks to get up from hibernation. Flowers don't have a calendared schedule for when they're supposed to bloom. Just us! He who "placed that star in a precise orbit millennia before it appeared over Bethlehem in celebration of the birth of the Babe has given at least equal attention to placement of each of us in precise human orbits," Neal A. Maxwell.

For example, when we see a life ending too soon and claim unfairness and injustice, let us remember that our Father also decided when that brother or sister of ours, or son or daughter, should join us here on Earth (birth) and is simply bringing them home in accordance with those heavenly timetables that reach far beyond our grasp of comprehension.

Tanner Hollingsworth is a dear friend of mine, a beautiful soul who fell into that nearly impossible category of understanding…*those who left us too soon*. Tanner was a newly married father with an adorable little two-year-old son and twin boys who were due in a matter of weeks. His sweetheart of a wife, Courtney, was devastated as her beloved husband of less than one year, suddenly, without warning and with still no explanation regarding cause of death, passed from this life and on to the next.

I had the absolute honor, privilege and sheer burden of officiating at Tanner's funeral. Having coached Tanner over the previous year and his mom for three years, they entrusted me to stand before a crowd of nearly three hundred who had come to pay tribute to an outstanding human. It took everything I had to hold myself together, while also holding space for all who were grieving. Angels were strengthening many that day. I was eternally grateful to be a recipient of that celestial assistance.

In my closing remarks, I looked down from the stage at the grieving family on the front row, yearning for answers, peace of mind, anything to bring a little hope. As my gaze carefully scrolled past his broken-hearted parents, wife, little boy and siblings, I had a powerful witness come over me and I spoke out loud what I knew to be true in my heart and mind: "This man will do things for your family far beyond the bounds of mortality. He will be involved in your lives as a ministering angel untethered by earthly constraints."

In the months that followed, Tanner's family spoke of sacred experiences with me, too personal to share publicly, of the miraculous fulfillment of those spoken words. They clung to the belief that Tanner was indeed and always would be a present and powerful influence in their lives.

Brought back home, Tanner is now able to drive roots, without restraints, to his Source. And once tapped into that Source, the power to bring forth abundance to others' lives is infinite, and he keeps showing up in that way. None of us understood it, his heavenly timetable, and yet we've all had to come to grips with it, Tanner most of all. What's beautiful is to feel, undoubtedly, that he is.

We often say, "May he rest in peace." I know Tanner has never been one to sit back when there's a great work to be done. I know his presence lovingly lives on in all of us, impacting each of us, touching our hearts and minds. Tanner continues to plant seeds…and even now is doing so in my life and in yours as I share some of the impact he has had in my existence. Tanner, keep plowing forward, my friend, and may your roots always bear great fruit!

This is a book about strength. And the amazing thing about strength is that there's no limit to its capacity especially when you dig your roots in deeply to your Source. It can always increase, as Jesus taught through his life lived in crescendo.

Daniel James Brown shared in his book, *The Boys in the Boat*, that George Yeoman Pocock, the incomparable handcrafter of boats and men, "talked about the underlying strength of the individual fibers in cedar and how, coupled with their resilience, they gave the wood its ability to bounce back and resume its shape, whole and intact, or how, under steam and pressure, they could take a new form and hold it forever. The ability to yield, to bend, to give way, to accommodate, he said, was sometimes a source of strength in men as well as in wood."

You have that strength within you. He's not just talking about college aged young men who are entering the prime of their lives. It runs through every fiber of *your* body, mind and soul. *You* were created to bounce back and resume the shape that God intends for you to be. **Strength of the Willow**.

You have a remarkable resilience that pulls you to be whole and complete, perfect, as the Greek word so aptly describes from Jesus' Sermon on the Mount. **Strength of the Oak**. And under life's inevitable pressures, *you* can grow into a beautiful form that is waiting to be filled, a form that can last forever. *You* can yield, bend, give way, accommodate as you tap into your truest inner resolve and live a principle-based life. **Strength of the Willow.**

You have a deep, inner fortitude waiting to express itself that is far greater than the **Strength of the Oak** or the **Strength of the Willow**.

Rudyard Kipling penned exquisitely poetic words which sum up, better than any others I've ever heard, what it takes to exude this kind of strength. I share a portion of them with you here and invite you to study the entirety in another setting.

If
If you can keep your head when all about you
Are losing theirs and blaming it on you,
If you can trust yourself when all men doubt you
But make allowance for their doubting too…
And yet don't look too good, nor talk too wise…

This encompasses such a grounded, individual power. Knowing we are who we are and owning our own stuff and letting go of everyone else's is not an easy thing to do. And then keeping our humility in the process…genius! **Strength of the Willow.** Kipling also shares the required mindset for staying strong amidst the ups and the downs that are unmistakably inevitable.

> *If you can force your heart and nerve and sinew*
> *To serve your turn long after they are gone,*
> *And so, hold on when there is nothing in you*
> *Except the Will, which says to them, 'Hold on!'*

To me, this is all about resilience, the payoff for being all in, committed no matter what. It takes a knowingness, a clarity of purpose, a Life Mission so substantial that giving up is out of the equation. **Strength of the Oak**. And then, Kipling packs in a final word for the wise:

> *If you can talk with crowds and keep your virtue,*
> *Or walk with Kings—nor lose the common touch,*
> *Yours is the Earth and everything that's in it,*
> *And—which is more—you'll be a Man, my son!"[56]*

Man or woman regardless, you are a child of God, and have the power to create an amazingly impactful life for yourself and the kings and commoners you choose to bring into your world. Remembering the principles of the **Strengths of the Oak, Strengths of the Willow,** and strengths of the Savior can bring power, balance and virtue into any life.

Journal Entry 🖊 *What change is needed most for you to develop both oak and willow-like strength in your life right now? How do you plan on making that happen? What tools will you use from this book to guarantee the success of your plan? What will you see, hear, feel, etc. when this plan unfolds?*

---

[56] See appendix for full version of this poem.

CHAPTER FIFTEEN

Bringing Heaven to Earth
and Earth to Heaven

"Some people are so heavenly minded
that they are no earthly good."
—Oliver Wendell Holmes

When I was a teacher, I understood the importance of leaving a lasting first impression upon the minds and hearts of those hungry teenage kids. During the first week of school, I did everything I could to set a positive and powerful tone for the rest of the semester. One of the memorable lessons I always taught on the last day of that first week was entitled, *The World's Greatest Class,* and the students just ate it up. . .literally.

As they entered the classroom, they found a long table at the front covered with a blanket. It was nearly impossible to decipher what, exactly, was underneath the covering. There were some large, bulky items and the students would ask if they could peek. I always had to shoo away a few pesky hands from trying to do so.

After the bell rang and we'd all settled in, some simply couldn't take it anymore as their curiosity was killing them. I milked this for what it was worth until finally, in dramatic fashion, like the unveiling of a grand masterpiece, I'd slowly remove the covering to reveal a large mixing bowl and a laundry basket full of ingredients and baking supplies. As I pulled down on the projection screen and let it roll itself up toward the ceiling, the following words were revealed, written on the whiteboard, in my fanciest cursive, of course:

The World's Greatest Class

I'd pull on my apron and tie it in the back. Then, I'd cross out the word "class" and write the word "cookies," so it now read: *The World's Greatest Cookies*. "Today, we're baking cookies! Who'd like to be my baking assistant?" Hands flew up faster than a wig in a windstorm.

After calling on an energetic and eager volunteer I'd say, "Please turn to a blank page and write *Recipe for the World's Greatest Class* at the top. We're baking cookies for the next hour. Let's liken the ingredients and steps of baking chocolate chip cookies to key ingredients and steps we can take to create the greatest classroom experience you've ever had."

To me, it seems like just about all teenagers love cookies, so the following sixty minutes were full of fun and laughter, coupled with powerful insights and commitments for our next four or five months together. There was always one or two in every class that took some warming up, a bit of persuading to get *everyone* on board. By the end of the hour though, they were all engaged.

As they wrote down the ingredients for the cookies, they'd also come up with classroom comparisons. For example, I'd say, "What purpose do eggs serve in the recipe?" This one often stumped them. I'd follow up with, "Eggs solidify when cooked and hold all these other things together, right? So, what can we do in here that will solidify us as a class and help bring all of us together?" That's when these kids would shout out things like:

- Participation
- Getting to know each other
- Being respectful of everyone's perspectives

It was fun to watch the students' eyes grow big and disbelieving as I'd also pretend to toss in some undesirable ingredients—egg shell, motor oil, mustard or a cup of salt. Let me tell you, the reaction you can get out of a hungry teenage boy when you're about to desecrate chocolate chip cookie dough is priceless! We'd then compare that nasty, uncalled for "ingredient" with things that could, and would, absolutely destroy the learning environment. Their list included:

- Mocking each other's opinions
- Uncalled for sarcasm
- Texting or games or social media on their phones during our time committed to learning

At the very end I'd ask, "Who loves the dough more than the actual cookies?" I'd call up a student to have a taste and invite them to confirm that this probably was one of the greatest recipes they'd ever tasted. As the student walked away, I'd pick up the bowl of dough and hold it over the garbage can. Slowly, carefully, I began tilting the bowl as if I were ready to throw all of our delicious concoction into the trash. Several audible gasps and often a "NOOO!" would be heard. That bottomless pit of a teenage boy's stomach would propel him out of his seat and into his role as the hero of the class as he flew forward to salvage the sweet creation. Keeping his unkempt and unwashed hands out of the bowl was my motivation, so I'd always make sure to only tease as if the dough was actually falling.

After reassuring him and the rest of the class that I wouldn't dare do something so absurd, I'd say, "Now, how sad would it be if we *did* throw away all of this tasty cookie dough? Wouldn't it be a pity to not bake and partake of our hard work today?" I let this sink in to all the nods with a pause. "So, how can we liken this to our learning here in our classroom?"

After a brief moment of reflection, a lightbulb would soon go off and a perceptive student would respond, "Well, it would be like us having these great experiences together and feeling motivated to make changes in our lives and then going back to the real world and not applying what we've learned. So many times we feel it in *here* and forget it out *there*. We can't do that. We can't throw this dough away!"

Bingo!

At this moment, I'd have my wife walk in (assuming we timed it perfectly between the class period's ending and the little girl's naps at home) with a freshly baked tray of warm, gooey, succulent chocolate chip cookies, the heavenly smell wafting into the room the second the door was opened. Ready to be ravished by the drooling mouths of twenty or thirty students, those cookies would never last more than mere seconds. So, while I had their full attention, I said this:

"Now, if you promise me that you will do everything in your power to apply the principles we'll be studying, to live the commitments you make and internalize all of our learnings this semester into your daily lives *outside* of our classroom, then you can have a cookie."

They were sold.

From then on, those kids started to expect hot cookies in every class (not just mine). Some of the other teachers didn't really appreciate that, but I knew how powerful the lesson was and that was a risk I was more than willing to take. I never had a negative reaction no matter how many times I used it.

I really wish I could knock on your door right now, while you're reading, with a plate of freshly baked cookies in hand and make the same deal with you. Just like those high schoolers, wouldn't it be sad if *we* threw away all of *our* learnings, the changes we've felt inspired to make, the tools we've acquired together and the example of Jesus and our higher purpose we've unpacked?

Congratulations, you got through the book!

But, did the book get through to you?

You see, learning is not what happens in the classroom of these pages or even in the thoughts in your mind or the feelings of your heart. It's what you do with all of this that matters. Learning is the planting of the seed while your hands are breaking the ground. It's the patience of waiting. **Strength of the Willow.** It's the determination and commitment to keep on watering. **Strength of the Oak.** Learning is the growth that takes place while your stress wood develops through life's hellish storms. Learning is your change of behavior, your evolving character, your consecrated humanness— and I mean *consecrated*.

I'm asking you to take a massive bite, internalizing what you've experienced as you've read this book. Apply what you now have and let it change you from the inside out. Go back into our world with this newly blossomed fruit, this elixir of life and share it...*please* share it. Wake up and challenge each day with your Life Mission in hand.

In fact, will you please go back to p. 36 and look at what you wrote regarding your Life Mission? How does it feel to you? Does it light you up? Does it deliver a punch of passion and excitement? Does it make you want to get up and get going with a grand symphony accompanying your departure? Is there a sense of urgency when you read it? Do you feel compelled to move immediately in the direction of its fulfillment? Are you enthused by the possibilities that could come as you pour yourself into achieving what you wrote?

If the answer is 'yes,' then it's time to go serve someone!

If the answer is 'no,' would you be willing to accept a challenge from me? Go serve someone! I'm serious. Chad Hymas rocked my world years ago with this same challenge. As you now accept it from me, you will discover your unique calling to carry it out as well. It's there, hidden outside of you as a quest, beckoning your very best. Go get it! Embody it. Make it yours. Own it. Carve it in stone. Watch the magic manifest.

Bring that Life Mission home and lead your family with sturdy lateral roots, values and principles that must be passed from generation to generation. If you don't, who will? Show up in your workplace or your business with a new vision of powerful accountability, intentionality and creativity. Influence your community and our world with Christ-like commitment and God's grace empowering you every step of the way.

Move *toward* what you want. Think about my little boy Brody on his bike. "Look at the tree. Keep pedaling." Be all in, like my friend John, and buy a one-way ticket to wherever your soul is beckoning you to go. Burn the ships if needed. Don't come down from *your* great work, like Nehemiah. And once you've got the momentum, ride hands free! Let go and let God take you on an unforgettable ride! Freedom is yours.

Continue to create space for joy in every single aspect of your life. No one gets to choose what you hold onto but you. If it doesn't feed your faith, cut it out! Play to win. Build a world-class Rat Park that's so exciting, there's no room for mediocrity. Be, do and have everything you can imagine, counting the cost and making appropriate plans. Be intentional, and when needed, intentionally unintentional to preserve your natural strengths. Unstring the bow so you will be ready when it's required.

Let loose the courageous and compassionate person that your Divine Parents intended you to be by fully living in a beautiful swing state, that plane on which champions row. In this state of flow, humbly accept and enjoy the essence of *all* you were destined to be. And if you fall in the water, laugh at yourself! Do it again. Fail forward faster. Forgive yourself and everyone else that may have tipped the boat. Make that choice ahead of time, before you ever get in it. Declare each day: "No matter what, I forgive." Do it out loud. We need to hear your voice. And when things just are not going your way and you want to curse the cosmos, trust instead—trust those heavenly timetables.

Above all, I want you to know this: you can bring this piece of heaven to Earth. All you've got to do is ground yourself to your Source and let that taproot nourish every ounce of your being. Drive the deepest, strongest roots you can and grow the grandest wings possible and simply watch—watch what happens when you unleash superhuman powers that defy all description. Remember, being grounded, even when and *especially* when you're at rock bottom, is an imperative part to the process for your personal growth. Do not curse the grounding. Lean into it. Embrace it. Give gratitude as you bring meaning to your suffering and purpose to your unique and at times pain-filled path.

Love every moment, every day. This doesn't mean you have to *like* all of it. And yet, you can love it. You can respect it and graciously transform it. Use the gift of each sunrise to fuel why you're here and what you're all about. Greet the good, the bad, the unexpected ugly and befriend every situation as potential for something spectacular that's unfolding for you.

This is where strength comes from. *You* are that strength. *You* are the connection between heaven and Earth. *Your* presence is enough; no, it's more than enough to accomplish all that God needs done, even in our turbulent world. Choose the badge of courage that is proudly worn when you boldly bear the unequivocal **Strength of the Oak.**

Carry the cradle of compassion that caresses the undeniable **Strength of the Willow.** The poetic synergy and powerful compound of these extraordinary strengths are yours. The world is waiting for *you*.

You've got over a dozen meticulously crafted tools, right here at your fingertips, that I've provided for your success. Just like any new tool or toy, our mastery and enjoyment come as we put it to use. The more we practice and play with it, the greater our proficiency and pleasure. Take a look at what you now have:

- Life Mission
- Values for each area of your Wheel of Life
- Your Personal Playbook for Guiding Life Principles
- 4 Steps of Applied Gratitude (Scuba Style)
- Losing Labels and Affirming Who You Truly Are
- Dropping Ego Questions
- Your Rat Park
- The Rule of 3
- 411 Worksheet
- Weekly 411 Meeting
- Daily Calendar Calibration
- Swing State GPS or 1-3-5
- Formula for Self-Reliance
- 7 Proven Steps to Forgiveness of Others and Yourself
- 7 Solid Steps for Asking Others for Forgiveness

I challenge you to revisit these in one week from today. Go ahead and put a reminder in your calendar right now. Come back and remind yourself of what you've learned and make sure you're utilizing these powerful mechanisms that have been designed to transform your life. Set another reminder to look at these again in one month, next quarter, six months from now, and a year.

As you continue to evolve, your growth will require new levels of implementation with these tools. I know I can do a lot more with a screwdriver in my late thirties than I could when I was three! And so it will be with you and what I've gifted you in this book. But you've got to pick up the tools; it's the only way to ensure that what you've come to love and learn about yourself and your purpose in life will manifest into your continued growth and development.

Also, please share this wealth of knowledge! The hand that's open to give is the hand that's open to receive. In giving away what we've gained, we solidify our ownership of priceless principles. Teaching what we've recently read strengthens our grasp on newly acquired gems. As you invite others to dive into this book, you'll have a trusted tribe who will be there to support and encourage your personal improvement. The journey of learning is smoother, faster, brighter and way more fun when we bring those we love along for the ride.

Case in point: one client, a dear friend and sister in my tribe, came to me after already having years of highly successful rises in her life. Most people, from the outside looking in, would have said, "Heather's arrived! That girl's got it made." This is a woman who I looked up to as a mentor and role model long before she asked me for help. She was showing up as an admired leader in her industry, a force to be reckoned with. So, you can imagine my surprise when she turned to me, desperate for a breakthrough.

One of the coaching experiences I've become renowned for is what I call a Breakthrough Session. During this deep dive, we discover how your mind has conditioned you to be where you're at in your Wheel of Life and what's preventing you from total fulfillment. We spend five or six hours, over two days, releasing all of your negative emotions and limiting beliefs.

While Heather knew she was rocking it in many aspects of her professional field, social life and family, she was struggling with something so deeply buried from childhood, it was affecting her physical body and her spirituality. This was beginning to bleed out into other areas of her life, and she needed what she'd come to see I offered.

I was humbled and honored, ready to go to work for this spiritual warrior who had been so vitally influential in my own journey.

In her open and tender manner, Heather just couldn't ignore the call that was quickly turning into a shout in her mind. It was time to tear up and out of her comfort zone of greatness, which was becoming more and more uncomfortable with every passing day. She could clearly see what God was inviting her to be and do, a new and dynamic adventure into her zone of genius. But she was stuck.

Heather surrendered. She *gave over* her will to God because she recognized that going at it alone was a risky way to approach such a bold and daunting feat.

As we embarked into our six-hour session, I could feel something magical was about to happen for Heather. Opening up and learning all about her intensely ingrained patterns, dark emotions and betraying beliefs brought a welcomed awareness. Heather already knew she had been sexually abused as a child and threatened with her life if she told. She was completely aware of wounds she had experienced from first being abandoned before being adopted into a kind and loving family. However, despite all of her deep, inner work, she did not know how all of her unconscious beliefs, formed as a child, had so tightly woven together in her framework of self-understanding.

Now as she was getting ready to level up into a new and bold challenge in her life and career, Heather was hiding. It was now blowing up in her face in the form of a health crisis. For some reason, when money, health and safety all came together, she was as frozen as that little girl in her beliefs about herself. Through my process, the eyes of her understanding renewed her realization as to how she'd become lodged into this damning crevice. With a magnificent peak in sight, this path that proved to produce such extraordinary success had also led her to this place of temporary captivity.

In respecting this painful, forward fall instead of ignoring it, Heather received a gift—a beautiful appreciation and profound gratitude for what was hidden in the ashes. She now held a precious gem of love, a magnificent treasure that beamed from her hands and heart with a **Strength of the Willow** light for all to behold. There was also a phoenix-like fire that was rising. It was a **Strength of the Oak**, bodacious prowess into a glorious new level of possibility for world-wide impact. As I walked beside her, it all unfolded before her.

She's doing it. Her stage is Universal. Heather has brought heaven down to Earth. She is fulfilling the measure of her abundant creation as she brings us closer to the Divine. Her legacy continues to expand as she, in her own unique, unrepeatable miracle kind of way, is transforming countless lives around us. She's leveraging her past, and that of all who hear her message, to discover and create a most incredible destiny. And if Heather were here with you and me right now, she'd tell you to take the biggest, most delicious bite possible out of everything life has laid before you. No egg shells in her recipe!

Think about this: what if Heather had not asked for my help?

One Final Journal Entry 🖊 *What are you not asking for, which, if you were to receive, would have a massive impact on your Life Mission?*

Go out and ask for whatever it is or whoever it might be that will fuel your Life Mission. Go get it!

Now, I've delivered the proverbial cookies, and I want to hear what *you're* doing with them. I promised I'd share my email, and I really do want to hear about your grounding, strengthening, sacrificing, consecrating and transformative experiences.

Your stories light me up! Please reach out to me, anytime at ***andrew@ andrewLanderson.com*** or on social media ***@andrewLanderson85***. And if you'd like to bring me onboard as your business or life transformational coach or keynote speaker for your next great event, I'd be honored to have the opportunity. Shoot me an email or visit me at ***andrewLanderson.com***.

Onward and upward, my friend.

> *"Aim at Heaven and you will get Earth 'thrown in': aim at Earth and you will get neither."*
> —*C.S. Lewis*

Personal Gratitudes

If you show me these three things, I'll know just about everything I need to know about any given person: 1) their calendar 2) their bookshelf 3) the five people they spend the most time with. I wish I could say it was just five, and yet I am who I am today, an author, because of these beautiful souls...

Bridget Cook-Burch, you are the only person on the planet who could summon the power to pull out the **Strength of the Oak** and **Strength of the Willow** from the deep, fibrous parts of *my* stress wood. Your relentless, loving belief in me and fierce coaching brought inspiration into being. I had no idea what was possible before meeting you. And thank you for bringing Hannah Lyon, the mighty one, into my world as a most meticulous and visionary editor. Hannah, you are the magic in the white parts of the page.

The Inspired Legacy Publishing team along with the cohort of publishing and media magicians at RHG Media Productions, especially Rebbeca Hall Gruyter, you kept this all together and created a beautiful symphony for us to enjoy. Rebecca, your persistent patience along with such warm and welcoming grace were exactly what I needed.

Kevin Hall, your mentorship in teaching me how to teach others how to fish is indeed changing civilizations. You were the first person I called when I answered my call to write this book. I appreciate your words of powerful wisdom. Namaste, my brother.

Seth Jacobsen, the challenge that sounded something like this: "Andrew, you need to write a book!" will forever grow brighter and more valuable in my memory bank. You saw what the world needed that I had to offer. Thank you for planting the seeds of possibility.

Karey Hunter and Katie Mandler, your "Amen, Seth!" and support meant more to me than you'll ever know. Thank you for trusting me and pushing me to greater heights. You were some of the greatest "wingmen" I could have ever had. I will always cherish our time together and friendship.

Derek Sell, John van der Giessen, Luke Gilbert, David Bingham, my best friends. Each of you has played a key role in loving me, stretching me, holding space for my growth and modeling distinct and unique character strengths that I richly admire.

Erica Hill and Stacie States, you took a chance on me. You dug the well that gave me the life to lead others. Thanks for letting me into your three-foot bubble.

Derek Schenck, Ron Patulski, Micah Fox, David Scoggins, Dianna Kokoszka, you were the coaches who showed me what care and candor are all about. Your examples of masterful coaching helped me break through any limiting beliefs that I had regarding my potential to live out my Life Mission. I could write a book on each of you.

My seminary brothers who put up with a punk kid (me), Adam Cobb, Doug Richens and Trevor Bell. Your Christ-like love and example have stayed with me well beyond the classroom. That cookie lesson, your dance moves and desks covered in shaving cream opened my eyes to what's possible when we authentically connect with each individual. I love you and thank our Heavenly Father for your place and time in my world.

Brett Ferrin, Todd Baird, Rand Martel and Randy Rhoton, I'm literally in tears thinking about sitting at your compassionate feet. You brought me out of the darkest days of my life. You breathed hope back into my spirit. Repentance—a change of mind, a fresh view of God, myself and the world—came from your benevolent counsel. All my love!

My Canadian and Belgian brothers from other mothers, Richard Haynes and Xavier Istace, you were the first to read my book and kept me going all along the way. God knew I needed you both. No words can do justice.

My hometown sisters who adopted and befriended me and brought me into your homes, lifting my spirits through selfless service, Whitney Fredin and Valerie Dumas. The meals, hanging out, listening and asking meaningful questions, your kindness and empathy kept me afloat.

All of my students and clients who have trusted me to learn along-side you, I have received so much from your life experiences. Thanks for being my guinea pigs!

My teachers, coaches, friends, neighbors, coworkers, mission companions and classmates from Frontier Elementary School to the Hickories Subdivision and everywhere in between, you have all left your impressionable mark of goodness on my heart. The world needs you now more than ever.

Mom and Dad, you are the oak and the willow all wrapped into one. Thank you for planting, nurturing, pruning and most importantly, being patient with my progress. I know I've helped you gain more stress wood than the other four that came before. You're welcome ;)

The "A Team," my older brother, Adam, and three older sisters, Mandy, Aleesa and Angie, you are my first line of defense, the angels that led the way and set the example for me to follow. I couldn't have asked for a better starting line-up.

My perfect-for-me companion, Chari, and my beautiful children, Kella, Taycee, Avery, Brody, Taylen and Jacob, you are the most important people in my world. I love you. Each day, I pray for your happiness and thank Heavenly Father for the joy you are in my life.

About the Author

Everybody yearns to have at least one person in their life who believes in them; that they can do what they say they can do, who believes they can be the person they want to be. Andrew is that person.

Andrew grew up in an idyllic (and far from perfect) suburban home in Boise, Idaho with parents who exuded unconditional love toward him and his four older siblings. He learned valuable life lessons from Little League baseball to an early morning paper route. After high school, Andrew attended college and went on a two-year service mission for his church to Alabama, Belgium and France. He made forever friends with people from all across the globe and came home fluent in French and decent in Spanish. These were formative years for Andrew, solidifying his desire to commit to his Life Mission, to bless his brothers and sisters, who are God's children, to live a higher level of spiritual strength. It is to influence as many as possible.

Completing an undergraduate degree in Communication and a master's degree in Education, the high school classroom was a perfect fit in launching a career of teaching, influencing and leading. This is where he truly found his voice and inner drive to bring out the best in those who landed on his path.

Since 2015, Andrew has cultivated this passion as a best-selling author, speaker and coach, helping individuals break through limiting beliefs, transform their lives and businesses and find lasting freedom. In 2017, he built and led a coaching team as they grew one of the largest and most successful Keller Williams Realty Productivity

Coaching Programs in the nation. With 116 active clients at the time, The Productivity Team became a head-turning leader in the field of real estate coaching.

Empowering his agents through goal setting, business and life planning, mastering sales skills and overcoming limitations prepared Andrew to be selected as a national coach with KW MAPS Coaching. This journey led him to become certified with the Association for Integrative Psychology as a Master Practitioner of Neuro-Linguistic Programming (NLP) and a Master Practitioner in Mental and Emotional Release Therapy. From that point on, he began coaching the top business minds, leaders and coaches in an elite form of Transformational Coaching.

Today, Andrew continues to pour his passion into keynote speaking as well as coaching business owners, entrepreneurs, sales people, artists, coaches and consultants all around the world. He also loves giving of his time through mentoring youth and young adults as they launch into a happy and healthy trajectory for their future.

When he's not at work, you can find him with his family on the soccer field, basketball court, dance/piano/violin/guitar recital halls, the ski lift, mountain bike trails or backpacking the beautiful mountains of Idaho. His wife and kids drive his Life Mission and in return, that mission provides an abundant life for their family.

At the end of the day, know this: Andrew will take a stand for your greatness more than you will stand for your own limitations. He will fight harder for your possibilities than you do. If you're ready to break through and find unprecedented strength, please reach out to **support@andrewLanderson.com** or keep up with other opportunities at **andrewLanderson.com** or on social media **@andrewLanderson85**.

Appendix

- Life Mission (p. 36)
- Values for each area of your Wheel of Life (p. 51)
- Your Personal Playbook for Guiding Life Principles (p. 65)
- 4 Steps of Applied Gratitude (Scuba Style) (p. 97)
- Losing Labels and Affirming Who You Truly Are (p. 102)
- Dropping Ego Questions (p. 109)
- Your Rat Park (p. 119)
- The Rule of 3 (p. 125)
- Weekly 411 Meeting (p. 133)
- 411 Worksheet (p. 134)
- Daily Calendar Calibration (p. 136)
- Swing State GPS or 1-3-5 (p. 145)
- Formula for Self-Reliance (p. 153)
- 7 Proven Steps to Forgiveness of Others and Yourself (p. 169)
- 7 Solid Steps for Asking Others for Forgiveness (p. 171)

MY LIFE MISSION:

_____

_____

_____

_____

_____

_____

THE WHEEL OF LIFE

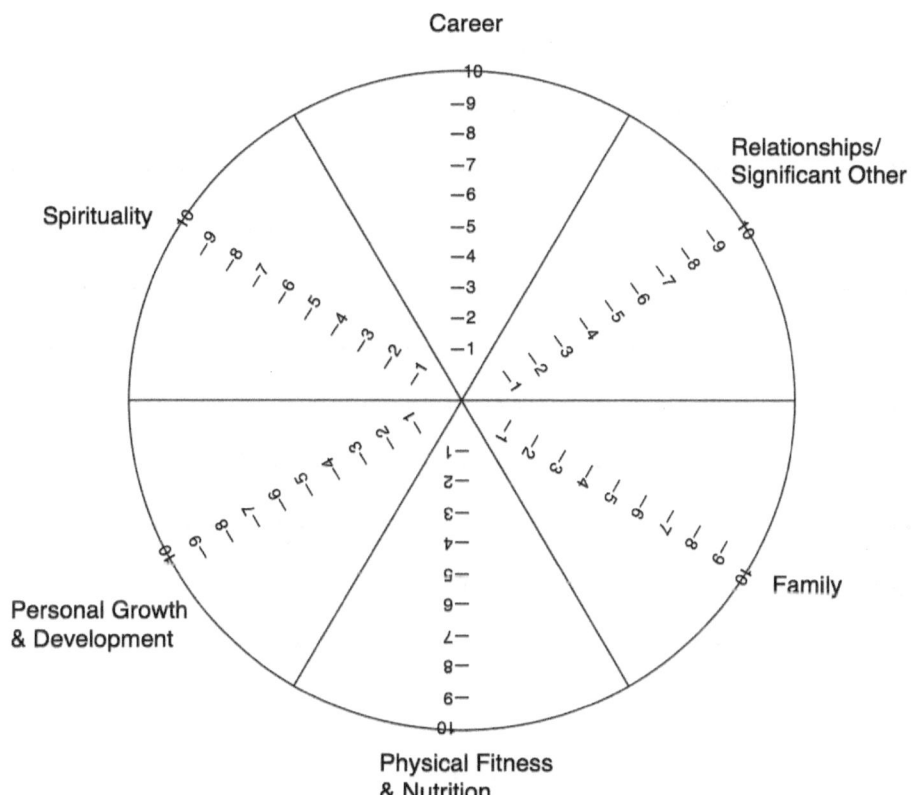

MY PERSONAL PLAYBOOK FOR SUCCESS:
GUIDING LIFE PRINCIPLES

4 STEPS OF APPLIED GRATITUDE

1. **Write down at least five gratitudes.**
2. **Why are you grateful for each?**
3 **Share this gratitude with at least one person.**
4. **Honor the One who gave you this person.**

LOSING LABELS: AFFIRMING WHO YOU TRULY ARE

→ **I am indeed powerful beyond measure!**

→ **I am brilliant, gorgeous, talented and fabulous!**

→ **I am a child of God (a great creator, divine love, a universal intelligence...you choose).**

→ **I was born to make manifest the glory of godliness that is within me.**

→ **I am free from fear and my presence automatically liberates others.**

DROPPING EGO QUESTIONS

— Is that true? Am I _____?

— (If needed) Is that 100% true? Am I 100% _____?

— (If needed) Is that all that I think I am?

— Aren't I more than that?

— So, what am I that's not _____?

— And beyond _____ (the word elicited in the previous question), is that all that I am?

— How much more am I than that?

— I do know I'm more than that, don't I?

— If desired, keep repeating the above questions and then end with, How do I know?

YOUR RAT PARK

#1 BE

As you look back on your life, what words would you use to describe who you've become over the years? What characteristics have you developed? How do others refer to you? What do you believe are the qualities that you will be remembered for? What do those who love you most and know you best say about your personality and your nature? Who have you become?

_____

_____

_____

_____

_____

#2 DO

What have you accomplished throughout your life? What did you do? Where did you go? Who did you serve? What kind of work were you passionate about? What was your impact on your family, friends, community, humanity? What skills did you acquire or master? What habits did you form? What talents did you develop and share? What special relationships did you cultivate? What did your life look like in action?

_____

_____

_____

_____

_____

#3 HAVE

What do you now have or did you have at one point? Did you finish that coin collection that meant so much to your grandfather? Did you take care of your mother's hand-crafted quilts? Did you finally restore your father's classic car? Did you share family memories in a vacation home, on a boat or in an RV? What did you have in your life that meant the world to you? What relationships do you have that are priceless? Think materially, relationally, spiritually. What gifts do you have or did you have at one time or another that you treasure? What have you acquired that is invaluable to you?

_____

_____

_____

_____

_____

THE RULE OF 3

1. **Internal Motivation (Do you *really* want it?)**
2. **System (Is there a system in place that is nearly fail-proof?)**
3. **Accountability (Who will best hold you accountable to this outcome?)**

Three simple keys that always seem to be present when success is in the air. And when goals aren't met and healthy habits are not formed, one or more of the three invariably seems to be missing.

I commit to holding a weekly 411 Meeting each _____ at ___:___

4-1-1 WORKSHEET

ANNUAL GOALS | YEAR

MONTHLY GOALS | MONTH OF

WEEKLY GOALS

WEEK 1	WEEK 2	WEEK 3	WEEK 4

MY 1-3-5

Goal or Desired Swing State:

_____

_____

Priority #1 _____

   1 _____

   2 _____

   3 _____

   4 _____

   5 _____

Priority #2 _____

   1 _____

   2 _____

   3 _____

   4 _____

   5 _____

Priority #3 _____

   1 _____

   2 _____

   3 _____

   4 _____

   5 _____

FORMULA FOR SELF-RELIANCE

An indomitable commitment to
our Life Mission, values and principles
+
Intentionality to create
the absolute best for our lives
+
The ability to move forward
making mistakes, laughing and being unintentional when appropriate
=
Grounded in a modern-day state that seems
to be losing numbers (self-reliance).

7 PROVEN STEPS TO FORGIVENESS
OF OTHERS AND YOURSELF

1. **Acknowledge and Assess:** Acknowledge the pain and assess the damage. What have you felt that hurts so badly? Name those emotions. What did you believe to be true about yourself because of this? What did you make this offense mean about you?
2. **See the Light:** What do you gain from holding on to all of this? Could you get this or something even better when you let go of the problem? What would you rather experience instead? What would life look like without this? What's the light at the other end of this dark tunnel?
3. **Get Permission:** Ask yourself for permission to be free. Are you open to the possibility of a better way? Allow yourself to say *'yes.'*
4. **Preserve the Learnings:** What do you need to learn from this experience, the learning of which will allow you to let go of the pain (the negative emotions or limiting beliefs)? Write this down. Preserve the positive learnings.

5. **Step into the Light:** How will this lightened load benefit you moving forward? What's possible now?
6. **Seal the Deal:** What actions do you need to take to really seal the deal and be 100% free to move forward? Do you want to approach the person or will a simple letter that can later be burned or deleted do the trick?
7. **Ensure Protection:** If you need to protect yourself from potential heartache in the future, set up safeguards by asking others to help. Decide what your boundaries are that you'll never cross again. Make a plan for protection.

7 SOLID STEPS FOR ASKING OTHERS FOR FORGIVENESS

1. **Admit:** Admit to yourself that a joyful life cannot unfold without taking care of this offense.
2. **Believe:** Believe that a Power beyond yourself can bring a restored peace.
3. **Decide:** Make a decision to turn this situation over to the care of God, your Source.
4. **Admit & Ask:** Admit to God the exact nature of your wrongs and ask for his help.
5. **Make Amends:** List out all persons who have been harmed because of the offense and, wherever possible, ask each person for forgiveness.
6. **Repair:** Do all that you can to right the wrong.
7. **Prevent:** Put parameters in place to protect yourself and others from having to deal with this similar situation in the future. Remember, it's better to prepare and prevent than to repair and repent.

If

If you can keep your head when all about you
Are losing theirs and blaming it on you,
If you can trust yourself when all men doubt you,
But make allowance for their doubting too;
If you can wait and not be tired by waiting,
Or being lied about, don't deal in lies,
Or being hated, don't give way to hating,
And yet don't look too good, nor talk too wise:

If you can dream—and not make dreams your master;
If you can think—and not make thoughts your aim;
If you can meet with Triumph and Disaster
And treat those two impostors just the same;
If you can bear to hear the truth you've spoken
Twisted by knaves to make a trap for fools,
Or watch the things you gave your life to, broken,
And stoop and build 'em up with worn-out tools:

If you can make one heap of all your winnings
And risk it on one turn of pitch-and-toss,
And lose, and start again at your beginnings
And never breathe a word about your loss;
If you can force your heart and nerve and sinew
To serve your turn long after they are gone,
And so, hold on when there is nothing in you
Except the Will, which says to them: 'Hold on!'

If you can talk with crowds and keep your virtue,
Or walk with Kings—nor lose the common touch,
If neither foes nor loving friends can hurt you,
If all men count with you, but none too much;
If you can fill the unforgiving minute

With sixty seconds' worth of distance run,
Yours is the Earth and everything that's in it,
And—which is more—you'll be a Man, my son!
—Rudyard Kipling

*This poem is in the public domain

Are you ready for a
MASSIVE
Breakthrough in *your* life?

Discover what's on the other side of your personal, professional and relationship challenges. It's time to break free and live your passion!

What's a Breakthrough Session?

Founded in the roots of Neuro-Linguistic Programming (NLP), we dive deep to discover how your mind has conditioned you to be where you're at in your life right now. We spend five-six hours releasing all of your negative emotions and limiting beliefs. You'll pick one area of your life to focus on, and all of that baggage will be gone! Then, we'll guide you through the SMART Goal process to set your focus and intention for the next twelve months.

Testimonials

After struggling with one particular area in my life, I asked Andrew for a Breakthrough Session. Within moments I came to realize how this "issue" was so intertwined with multiple areas of life, including

my business. What a marvelous, marvelous experience to be able to process and impact many erroneous beliefs in life and allow greater power, peace and passion to consume me again and set me on fire for life…and it's just beginning!"
—**Heather B.**

No matter how much our businesses have turned up our focus on sales, KPIs and effective habits of success, there always seems to be this level of interference building up inside. It can be the voice of doubt, the sting of temporary failure or the secret consideration of giving up. Andrew's method literally erases that as if it never existed…within two sessions! Imagine the power of running your business without that voice inside messing with you? It's possible and Andrew can make it happen! I believe every business person could do a Breakthrough Session one to two times a year and it would transform their sales, profit and retention like nothing else.
—**Seth C.**

I suffered from PTSD for several years as the result of watching my husband take his own life. There are no words to describe how our Breakthrough Session changed my world. I was given a second chance. Andrew guided me step by step through the process of MER to essentially reprogram my mind and heart. It's been more than a year now and I know I am forever free to live a life without triggers and fear! I cannot thank Andrew enough for helping me wake up every day full of love, joy, and excitement for my life!
—**Jenny P.**

Visit andrewLanderson.com to schedule your Breakthrough Session!

Transformational COACHING...
it's all about YOU!

Are you lacking a consistent system of support and accountability, someone or something to challenge your deepest potential? Transformational Coaching will launch this *journey* of purposeful change for you to fulfill your dreams, live out your values and achieve the results that matter...for you!

What is Transformational Coaching?

Fundamentally, it's about discovery, awareness and choice. It's a way of effectively empowering you to find your own answers, encouraging and supporting you on your path as you make important life-giving and life-changing choices. Coaching is not about solving problems, although problems will be solved.

After completing a Breakthrough Session, we focus on what you want—what you're creating in the next year and beyond. We have two sessions each month to hold you accountable and keep you moving toward your dreams and goals. The coach is there to help you live a life by design, a life of meaning and purpose.

Andrew listens intently and knows exactly what you need to help you get to the next level. He demands greatness, and you feel his care for you and what he's helping you accomplish. Couldn't be happier with the changes he's helped me make.
—Kara C.

Andrew's Proven Steps Series

Group Coaching Programs and Workshops

There's a feeling of freedom and empowerment that comes when we make a choice to be free from baggage and receive the greatest gift we can offer ourselves…Forgiveness…Love!

What's holding you back?

Based on the 7 Proven Steps to Forgiveness of Others and Yourself as outlined in this book, we spend eight weeks diving into the principles of forgiveness that have led hundreds to a place of peace.

This is a proven and powerful way to move beyond the past pain, be fully present to the enriching moments of right now and prevent unneeded hurt in the future. Once we've practiced and polished these seven steps, we can create an unconscious response of always forgiving, no questions asked, just like Mother Teresa, Gandhi, Nelson Mandela and Viktor Frankl.

You deserve this. Let's go… Visit andrewLanderson.com to sign up now for this and other courses

Reviews

Andrew L. Anderson's beautifully written book — *"Strength of the Oak, Strength of the Willow"* — teaches what courage looks and feels like and how, when it's bookended with compassion, we can fully commit to and fulfill our life's mission. The learnings and tools that you will acquire from reading and internalizing this written treasure will help you grow and truly live into your greatest potential.
— ***Kevin Hall, International best-selling author of "Aspire: Discovering Your Purpose through the Power of Words."***

"Absolutely one of my favorite personal development books of all time! *Strength of the Oak, Strength of the Willow* not only forces you to ask life's deepest questions about your purpose, but Andrew L. Anderson gives tools and challenges to learn how to fulfill it."
—***Bridget Cook-Burch, New York Times & Wall Street Journal Best-selling Author, Transformational Trainer & Passionate Humanitarian***

"Andrew is a man of depth, insight and wisdom; not just knowledge, but wisdom. There is a difference and if you dive into this book, you will see the difference. He makes the complicated simple; which is what great leaders do. He provides a well thought out and proven recipe for breaking destructive habits and plumbs the depths to show how transformation is truly possible."
—***Jake Proffitt, Kingdom Consulting LLC***

"Strength of the Oak, Strength of the Willow" is like a ray of sunshine for both mind and soul. Andrew L. Anderson invites us here to revisit our life mission. "To inspect what we expect," his unique recipe mixes simple yet powerful coaching tools based on his experience as both a leader and coach. It's a dose of philosophy, a subtle dusting of spiritual references and inspirational quotes. When you "let the book go through you," you just enjoy being guided to renew your values, your principles, and recommit yourself to divinely manifest your best existence.

—Sophie Rouméas, Mindful Therapies (Hypnosis & Systemic Constellation), Coach Mindfulness & Meditation

"Inspiration, self-reflection and hope...Strength of the Oak, Strength of the Willow delivers."

—Maureen Ryan Blake, Maureen Ryan Blake Media Productions

"This book is an outstanding teaching tool! The *Strength of the Oak, Strength of the Willow* is organized, contains questions that lead one to self-reflect, and has testimonials that are authentic. Andrew's ability to be vulnerable, seek feedback from others, and continually grow is inspiring! This book serves as a valuable resource to mentor and coach others."

—Deborah Wiener, Author, Speaker, Entrepreneur

"We spend so much time being scared of living and live on autopilot. Andrew has created a platform in which others can aspire to become more purposeful with courage and strength. Andrew puts his life experiences into perspective where the reader feels his integrity and leads by example."

—Seema Giri, #1 International Best-Selling Author, Leadership & Book Writing Mentor, Publisher & Podcast Host

"Andrew is a gifted coach and educator! The learnings and insights from his journey as a coach, leader, and Dad really resonated with me. The tools and the path forward that he shares are profoundly impactful! Viewing the world through the lens of the Willow and the Oak really creates a sense of grace and motivation through life. I'm excited to see how my attention and focus expand because of the process that Andrew has developed. Invest the time, read the book, commit to the exercise and watch divine intervention happen!"
—Melissa DeLuca, CEO of DeLuca & Willow, Co-Founder of Influence2Lead

"If you are ready to own your story and put yourself on a path of success and fulfillment, this book is absolutely for you. Andrew has convinced me that I am so much more capable of achieving my dreams than I ever thought was possible. I am walking away from this book feeling empowered because I have identified what is truly important to me, how I can push past any limiting beliefs, and how to make my dreams a reality. *Strength of the Oak, Strength of the Willow* will change your life. I guarantee it."
—Sadie Geddes, Saddie Geddes Fine Art

"This book will change your world if you let it, and I hope you will! Andrew is so relatable through his storytelling and gives detailed examples to easily follow. It feels like he's in the room coaching you to create and accomplish the life of your dreams."
—Haley Camp

www.ingramcontent.com/pod-product-compliance
Lightning Source LLC
Chambersburg PA
CBHW020236130626
46549CB00005B/1914